# GEORGE III
## A LIFE IN CARICATURE

KENNETH BAKER

With 194 illustrations

*George the Third*
*Should never have occurred.*
*One can only wonder*
*At so grotesque a blunder.*

Thames & Hudson

*For Stanley Kenneth Barclay,*
*our latest grandchild*

First published in 2007 in hardcover in the United States
of America by Thames & Hudson Inc., 500 Fifth Avenue,
New York, New York 10110

thamesandhudsonusa.com

Library of Congress Catalog Card Number 2007901128

ISBN 978-0-500-25140-9

Printed and bound in China by Everbest Printing Co.

*Half-title*   **A Bugaboo!!!**

2 June 1792

RICHARD NEWTON

*A royal proclamation of 21 May sought to prevent 'tumultuous meetings and
seditious writings'. Its target was Thomas Paine's writings and the radical
societies and clubs that had spread through London and the manufacturing
towns. Riots had broken out in Manchester and Sheffield over the high cost of
food and troops had to be called in. Richard Newton, a young satirist, attacks
the over-reaction of the government by depicting a clearly demented King as
the mouthpiece for the real architect of oppression, Pitt. George is made to
shriek out, 'Bristol Bastile! Birmingham Bastile! Manchester Bastile!
Informers! Confinement! Dungeons! Racks! Tortures! No Lenity!'*

*Frontispiece*   **St George and the Dragon**

2 August 1805

JAMES GILLRAY

*This is more like an historic tableau than a caricature. George becomes the
saviour of Britannia as he strikes down Napoleon. The threat of invasion was
at its climax. Crowned King of Italy at Milan in May, Napoleon returned to
France and in August visited his large army encamped at Boulogne, poised for
an invasion of England. The French Admiral Villeneuve, having fought an
indecisive battle against the English in July off Cape Finisterre, secured
reinforcements and headed south – to defeat in October at Trafalgar.*

*Opposite*   **His Most Gracious Majesty King George the 3rd**

1820

J. GEAR

*A silhouette on a black-bordered print, produced at the time of the King's
death in January 1820 after, the caption notes, a reign of 59 years, 3 months
and 9 days, one of the longest in English history.*

*p. 7*   **King George III and the Prince of Wales Reviewing The Prince Of
Wales's Regiment of Dragoon Guards and The Prince Of Wales's
Own Regiment of (Light) Dragoons** (detail)

*c.* 1797

ATTRIBUTED TO GEORGE BEECHEY AFTER WILLIAM BEECHEY

**A note on money conversions**

Some of the contemporary sums of money have been converted into today's
equivalent, so that the reader can have some sense of their magnitude. The
Office of National Statistics provides a retail price index going back to
medieval times. The rate of inflation in the period 1760–1820 increased from
6 per cent to 14 per cent. I have taken an average of 10 per cent. The index for
the base year of 2003 is 715.2. The amount of money is multiplied by that
index and divided by 10.

# CONTENTS

# PREFACE

GEORGE III AND HIS SON George IV lived through the golden age of caricature, which ran from approximately 1780 to 1830, and they suffered at the hands of Gillray, Rowlandson, Newton and Dent. Their caricatures were put up for sale in print-shop windows and as a result George III was the first monarch to be recognized by ordinary men and women in the street. In my book *George IV: A Life in Caricature* I explored his relationship with the caricaturists; in this book I deal with the more controversial and – at first glance – the less appealing figure of the father.

When George III ascended the throne in 1760 he was well liked, but twenty-one years later he was deeply unpopular, blamed for meddling in government and for losing the American colonies. In 1783, his sense of isolation and rejection was so great that he seriously contemplated abdication. Then an extraordinary transformation occurred, triggered by three events: the appointment of William Pitt as his Prime Minister in 1784; his recovery from his first bout of madness in 1788–89, which was welcomed by national rejoicing; and the French Revolution of 1789. With Europe confronting chaos and war, the stolid, unimaginative stubbornness of George became a virtue; the threat of a Napoleonic invasion in 1803 turned him into symbol of national resistance – a hero – and never was 'God Save the King' sung with such vigour and commitment.

All this is charted in the caricatures. Although Cromwell is said to have told his portrait painter Peter Lely to depict him 'warts and all', I doubt he would have extended such tolerance to the sort of scathing and scabrous prints that George III had to endure. For a time he became a laughing stock and there is even a glimpse of a bare royal bottom, but when British people can laugh at their monarchs they do not cut off their heads. Caricatures are one of the most vivid ways to learn about great historical figures and great events. They are snapshots capturing a moment in history and say more than columns of newsprint.

Most of the prints in this book are from my own collection but I have included some from public collections. I would like to thank Antony Griffiths, Keeper of the Department of Prints and Drawings at the British Museum; the Huntington Library in California; the Guildhall Library of the City of London and the Museum of London. Also special thanks to Kathleen Wright of the British Library; Sabrina Mackenzie of the Royal Collection; Oliver Preston for the use of prints from his own collection; and Benjamin Lemer who allowed me to use prints from his outstanding collecction of Richard Newton. I have once again had the invaluable help of Sara W. Duke, Curator, Popular and Applied Graphic Art, Prints and Photographs Division, in the Library of Congress. Sara is the loving custodian of the collection of 18th-century drawings and prints that was formed by George III and George IV. In a tragic error of judgement, the collection was sold by the Royal Library in 1921, for the paltry sum of £3,000. I have included several prints from that collection which are not in the British Museum. Most of the prints are in their original colours but a handful have been coloured at a later date.

I wish to thank John Wardroper, a fellow enthusiast and historian, for proofreading my text. I am also deeply indebted to Kathy Fogarty, my secretary, whose assistance has been essential and invaluable.

# Introduction

IN HIS *MEMOIRS*, the author Horace Walpole reported the death of George II on 25 October 1760: 'he rose as usual at six and drank his chocolate, for all his actions were invariably methodic. At quarter after seven he went into a little closet. His German *valet de chambre* in waiting heard a noise, and running in, found the King dead on the floor. In falling he had cut his face against the corner of a bureau. He was laid on a bed and blooded, but not a drop flowed: the ventricle of his heart had burst.'

Few mourned his passing and one politician noted that his funeral was 'not well attended by the peers and even the King's old servants'. George II had been more German than English and he was never happier than when visiting Hanover, which he did regularly. His heir was his 22-year-old grandson George, who was strong, good-looking and had led a life free from scandal. Above all, as the first king since James II to be born and raised in England, George III spoke English as his native tongue. Samuel Johnson, writing to a friend in Italy, reported, 'We were so weary of our old King that we are much pleased with his successor, of whom we are so much inclined to hope great things, that most of us begin already to believe them.'

Even Horace Walpole, no friend of the Hanoverian kings, could not forbear to cheer: 'His person is tall and full of dignity, his countenance florid and good natured, his manner graceful and obliging…I saw him yesterday and was surprised to find the levee had lost so entirely the air of the lion's den. The sovereign does not stand in one spot with his eyes fixed royally on the ground and dropping bits of German news. He walks about and speaks freely to everybody. I saw him afterwards on the throne, where he is graceful, sits with dignity and reads his answers to addresses very well.'

**A ticket for George III's Coronation at Westminster Abbey on 22 September 1761**

*George wanted to be married prior to his coronation. Protestant princesses, particularly from Germany, were discreetly looked over and suggested to him, and he finally settled on the obscure Charlotte of Mecklenburg-Strelitz, from a small duchy just south of Germany's Baltic coast. The seventeen-year-old Princess arrived at Harwich on 7 September and was married on the evening of the following day at St James's Palace. A fortnight later the King and Queen were crowned in Westminster Abbey. The celebration was conventional and rather modest: a short procession from Westminster Hall to the Abbey and then back for the coronation banquet. The public would not have seen much and Samuel Johnson wrote a pamphlet arguing for an extended route. George got the message and in November 1760 ordered a magnificent new state coach; it was ready for the State Opening of Parliament in 1762 and has been used on important occasions by succeeding monarchs ever since.*

You have got him Ma'am, in
the right Kew.

## You have got him Ma'am, in the right Kew

1768

*Even after eight years on the throne George, blindfolded, is being led by the nose by his mother, who gestures lewdly to Lord Bute hiding in the trees. The garden of Bute's house on Kew Green abutted that of the Princess Dowager of Wales and it led to many ribald comments about his erections at Kew. They were brought together by horticulture: Augusta created the Royal Gardens in the grounds of Kew, and Bute was later to publish significant books on flowers, shrubs and trees. Bute had been cut out of the King's circle in 1766 but the prints continued to cast George's mother as the evil influence behind the throne. In reality, her influence was exaggerated but she was both a target for those who wanted to attack the King and a scapegoat for his failings. James Townsend, a radical Lord Mayor of London, said on her death in 1772, 'The Princess Dowager of Wales was the real cause of all the calamities that have befallen this country for the last ten unfortunate years.'*

It was an auspicious time to ascend the throne. England was thrashing France in the Seven Years War and in 1759, the year of miracles, Wolfe had added Canada to the British Empire by beating Montcalm at Quebec. At home, the new machinery of the Industrial Revolution was beginning to make Britain the workshop of the world – as Edmund Burke commented: 'Commerce made to flourish through war.' In the countryside, where the majority of the population lived, a series of good harvests had spread contentment. Nonetheless, the euphoria was soon dissipated and by 1783 George III had become very unpopular; if he had died then, history would have written him off as an unloved political disaster.

During the 1760s George searched for a Prime Minister who would rise above the wrangling of Whig factions in order to sustain what was, after all, His Government. Then, through political misjudgement and military blunders, Britain suffered the humiliating loss of the American colonies, for which much of the blame was laid at George's door. The Methodist preacher John Wesley had discovered on his travels throughout the country in 1775 that 'the bulk of the people in every city, town and village do not much aim at the ministry…but at the King himself. They heartily despise his Majesty, and hate him with perfect hatred.' The records of the London theatres reveal that from George's accession to 1783 the song that was to become the national anthem, 'God Save the King', was sung only four times.

Yet all was to change again. Over the next twenty years the national anthem was sung hundreds of times as the people really did want God to save their King – he had became the patriotic leader of his country facing the threat of revolution and invasion. The key political change came in 1783 with George's appointment of the young William Pitt as his prime minister, the First Lord of the Treasury. He had at last found someone who was exceptionally competent, a dedicated workaholic, untainted by corruption, and in tune with his own ideas on how the country should be governed.

Even the cartoonists became a little kinder. He was portrayed as Farmer George, a genial, homely figure, and his parsimony, for which he had been much criticized, became a virtue in the light of the profligacy of his sons. His appalling illness in 1788–89 forged a bond between himself and his subjects; there was sympathy when the news leaked out, and heartfelt relief and national rejoicing when he recovered. During the bloody horrors of the French Revolution his stolidity became a positive virtue. Of all the European monarchs, George III emerged as the one who was most able to resist the revolutionary chaos that threatened to overwhelm Europe. He had become the nation's figurehead – a reincarnation of St George in one of Gillray's caricatures – and an embodiment of the national spirit needed to rally the country against the threat of an invasion by Napoleon.

This book charts the course of that extraordinary transformation, as seen through the eyes of the great caricaturists. Their prints were etched speedily and put up for sale in the windows of the print shops. For the first time many Londoners were able to see pictures, however distorted, of the royal family and leading politicians. George was always conscious of the majesty of kingship – he despatched official portraits of himself and Queen Charlotte to every part of the Empire – but it was through the caricaturists' prints that he came to be recognized by the public. Many of the prints ridiculed him and savaged his wife – in France their creators would have been imprisoned and even executed – but if people can laugh occasionally at their masters, they do not cut off their heads. It is unlikely that George would have laughed, as Henry Fox noted: 'His Majesty is not given to joke.' For the first twenty-three years of his reign, George could not have welcomed the prints but, as

they mellowed, they buttressed the monarchy, enhanced his reputation and endeared him to his people.

The change is reflected in two contrasting Scottish songs. One was written in 1786 by Robert Burns, who was no royalist, although he was later to work for the state as a Collector of Excise in Dumfries, and it had a sharp dig at his 'Sovereign King' for losing the American colonies:

> *Facts* are cheels [fellows] that winna ding [be shifted],
> An' downa [cannot] be disputed:
> Your *royal nest*, beneath *Your* wing,
> Is e'en right reft an' clouted [torn and patched]…

When Britain was threatened with invasion by the French in the 1790s, George's staying power was welcomed in a Dundee song:

> For under him we sit and crack,
> In peace and unity compact,
> Whilst every nation's on the rack
> That does nae like our Geordie.

After his illness of 1788–89 George was treated more sympathetically. Pitt served him well and the rancour and lack of confidence which had led him to dismiss two Prime Ministers and plot to bring down a third, were entirely absent. Events ran his way. The savagery of the French Revolution and the French declaration of war against England in 1793 brought out his best qualities: his dogged persistence; his modest way of living; his piety; and his devotion to a British victory. These endeared him to his people – his larger family.

George's role as head of his family is one of the keys to his complex character. The royal family was the most important in the country so it had to set an example and follow his direction – deviation was unacceptable. Rules had to be obeyed; standards were to be observed and conduct had to conform, and he suffered his greatest agony when time and time again his family let him down. His brothers – the Dukes of Gloucester and Cumberland – so damaged his sense of family by their secret marriages to English commoners that he expelled them from his presence; he told his mother, 'I shall have no further intercourse with them.' His sons appalled him by their extravagance, their lechery and their disobedience; and his daughters distressed him by their continual requests to marry Englishmen rather than German princes. His brothers', sons' and daughters' wish

**The Horse America, throwing his Master**

1 August 1779

*In 1778, the American War of Independence took a decisive turn when France, here depicted as a soldier carrying a fleur-de-lys flag, sided with the American rebels, and in 1779 Spain entered the war against Great Britain. The print predicts the ultimate defeat of Britain and the guilty man thrown by the stallion of America is George. Even after Cornwallis's surrender at Yorktown two years later George still believed that the war should go on. He said he had no doubt that 'when men are a little recovered of the shock felt by the bad news…they will find the necessity of carrying on the war'.*

to be independent reinforced George's stubborn insistence that they should bend to his will.

The more positive side to this relationship was that if a member of his family was threatened George would do anything to protect them. His sister Caroline Matilda, who in 1766 had married Christian VII of Denmark, was imprisoned in 1772 following her passionate affair with the court physician Johann Friedrich Struensee, who had dominated the mentally unstable King and briefly been the virtual ruler of Denmark. When George heard this he instructed the Earl of Sandwich, the First Lord of the Admiralty, to prepare a fleet to bombard Copenhagen if British demands for her release were not met. The Danish Court had to be made to realize that, 'Outrageous indignities to the Crown of England cannot pass with impunity.' It was the first time in English history that a king was prepared to threaten war in order to protect the honour of his sister. In the end, the Queen was allowed to go into exile in Celle, a town in the Hanoverian electorate.

By this time George's family was synonymous with the nation. In 1771, at the time of his dispute with his brother, Cumberland, a pamphlet, *Free Thoughts on Seduction, Adultery and Divorce*, declared boldly, 'A King of Great Britain is the master only of

his servants, he is, or ought to be, the father of his people, his subjects are his children.' George could not have described it better himself. For him, the nation, Empire and family were inextricably linked and he believed that he was accountable to God as head of his family, as king, and as ruler of the Empire. No other intermediary power could challenge his absolutism.

This lesson had in fact been learnt from his father, Prince Frederick, who had written a memorandum of advice for his ten-year-old son which he gave to his wife, Augusta, and which George carefully preserved among his papers. Frederick instilled into George's young mind that being a king of a nation was like being the head of a family, one made up of England, Scotland and Wales, and the Empire overseas. Family and nation were synonymous and rebellion, wilful disobedience and a lack of respect should not be tolerated, and punished if necessary. Prince Frederick was quite explicit: 'Convince the nation that you are not only an Englishman born and bred, but that you are also this by inclination, and that as you love your younger children next to the older, so you will love your other countries next to England.'

George took this advice to heart and looked upon the American colonies as part of his family, and therefore subject to his will. In September 1774, as the American Revolution came ever closer, George set out clearly what he perceived to be his duty: 'The colonies must either submit or triumph. I do not wish to come to severer measures, but we must not retreat. By coolness and unremitted pursuit of the measures that have been adopted I trust they will come to submit....I know I am doing my duty and can never wish to retract.' The last sentence illustrates one of the dominating commitments of George's life. He was utterly convinced that he had a duty, given by God and reinforced by his predecessors, but that last sentence could have been uttered by either Charles I or Cromwell.

In the ensuing war, which lasted until 1781, there were victories and defeats for the British. But at each setback George rallied his ministers, telling his Prime Minister Lord North not to flinch, and to redouble the efforts to bring the colonies to heel. For many Americans and particularly the drafters of the Declaration of Independence George was the villain – it was the King's War.

In June 1779, with the Government perpetually in crisis, George summoned the Cabinet to the Queen's House (now Buckingham Palace), where he 'declared to God he had never harboured the thought of injuring the Constitution or abridging his people's liberties'. He went on to tell them it was his duty to support his ministers and he now expected them to support him; it was his resolution 'to part with his life rather than suffer his dominions to be dismembered'. When the monarch so clearly set out his views how many ministers would be prepared to dissent? If they expressed even the slightest doubt about any policy they knew that they risked losing the favour and support of the King. Therein lay George's power and influence – for, after all, the government was the king's government.

After the humiliating surrender of Cornwallis at Yorktown in 1781, North paced up and down his room exclaiming, 'O God! It's all over.' But the King's speech a few days later did not concur, but without ministers to support him he had to recognize the humiliation of defeat: 'This completes the downfall of the lustre of this empire....Religion and public spirit are quite absorbed by vice and dissipation....I am innocent of the evils that have occurred.'

So great was George's sense of failure that on North's resignation in 1782 he contemplated abdicating and a year later he sat alone in the Queen's House to write out his abdication speech. In 1760, at the first parliamentary session of his reign, he had declared himself proud to be a Briton, but now he was preparing to retreat into that distant, unfamiliar, unvisited,

quiet land of his ancestors – Hanover. 'When I first appeared as your Sovereign in this place now above twenty-two years ago I had the pleasing hope that being born among you I might have proved the happy instrument of conciliating all parties.' Now, however, 'I am no longer of utility to this Empire. I am therefore resolved to resign my crown and all the dominions appertaining to it to the Prince of Wales, my eldest son and lawful successor, and to retire to the care of my Electoral dominions....For which purpose I shall draw up and sign an instrument to which I shall affix my private seal.'

But George did not do that. Who knew of this? With whom did he discuss it? There was no minister he could trust and he never discussed political issues with his wife or children. So, brooding alone in his palace, without any close friend to whom he could confide, he decided to put the speech among his papers and to remain king. Once again, he put duty above his personal inclinations and felt an obligation to ensure that the governance of his country did not fall into the hands of the Whigs, and in particular those of Charles James Fox. George saw it as his duty to bring down Fox, which he did, and in what turned out to be a stroke of genius he appointed William Pitt the Younger to be the First Lord of the Treasury, at the age of just twenty-four. The years of unpopularity were about to come to an end.

### Chatham's Ghost, or a Peep into Futurity. Che Sara, Sara

16 May 1780

*Lord North's government is tottering – the weathervane on the crown is pointing to the south. The ghost of the Earl of Chatham (who had died in 1778) is suffused in radiant glory and tells an alarmed George that they are all heading into the pit of chaos – a familiar design in prints. The damned are led by the Kings of France and Spain who were supporting the American rebels, followed by North carrying more tax demands, and Sandwich, First Lord of the Admiralty, bearing the news of the latest scandal at the Greenwich Hospital. Even a tired and exhausted Bute is dragged in. George treads torn county petitions underfoot. This was a low point in the reign: in April the House of Commons had passed a motion, as a rider to the consideration of the county petitions, demanding that the Crown's influence should be reduced.*

For the rest of his reign George interfered less. He had no significant involvement in Pitt's momentous decision to unite Ireland with the rest of Britain and he does not appear in any of the prints covering this issue. He did, however, intervene twice to protect the sanctity, as he believed it, of his coronation oath. This led to his dismissing Pitt in 1801 as well as the 'Ministry of All the Talents' in 1807 when they proposed to remove restrictions upon Roman Catholics. Those were two misjudgements but they were the last flicker of George's stubbornness. In the eyes of his subjects, George slowly became the father figure of his country – the very role he had written for himself. With Britain at war with France, the King became the symbol of national unity, respected, admired and even loved.

However, his bodily strength was slipping away. On three occasions, in 1788–89, 1801 and 1804, his life was clouded by periods of serious illness, now believed to have been porphyria. His eyes began to fail and he compensated for his deafness by shouting even more loudly. In 1810, at the age of seventy-two, George slipped into his final long, slow decline culminating in his death in 1820. In his last years he was confined to Windsor and, deserted by his wife and family, he lived there like a hermit. He played the flute, violin and harpsichord, sang, talked to ministers long dead and discussed affairs he never had. On occasion he had flashes of great clarity and one day said, 'I must have a new suit of clothes and I will have them black in memory of George III.'

CHATHAM'S GHOST, or a PEEP into FUTURITY.

George was still able occasionally to recall his hopes which had been dashed; his ambitions that were unfulfilled; the failure of his ministers and his generals; the happiness of his quiet family life at Windsor; and the disappointment of all his sons.

During a clearing of the clouds of memory he wrote his own epitaph: 'He was a good man.'

George III's reputation has undergone more changes than any other king in our history. The Whig historians dominant in the 19th century could not forgive him for bringing to an end, in the 1760s, the Whig ascendancy that had started in 1688. Their heroes were Chatham, Burke, Wilkes and Fox; the villain was George III, who aspired to be an absolute monarch. The fact that he suffered from 'madness' only reinforced his inadequacy in their eyes, and he was held to be largely responsible for the loss of the American colonies.

It was only in the mid-20th century that a reassessment began, pioneered by the researches of Sir Lewis Namier into the intricacies of the politics of the 1750s to 1770s. It was now considered too simplistic to divide parliamentarians into blocks of Whigs and Tories, and it was realized that George had faced real problems in marshalling majorities for his governments from the medley of interests in the Commons and the Lords. Namier's disciples became apologists for George. The King could not be held responsible for the loss of the American colonies since he did what a constitutional monarch should do: he supported Lord North, his Prime Minister, and the rights of Parliament to tax and govern the colonies. Could a king do otherwise?

The rehabilitation continued with the play by Alan Bennett, *The Madness of George III* (1991). Here the King was depicted as suffering from an undiagnosed hereditary disease for which he received treatment that was little short of torture. The human face of George III evoked sympathy and his recovery from 'madness' was greeted with as much joy in the 1990s as it had been in 1789.

### The Windsor Milkman; or, any thing to turn a Penny

12 June 1792

RICHARD NEWTON

*George in his staccato style is offering his milk for sale, 'Milk, ho! Milk, ho! Milk, ho! Come my Pretty Maids, tumble out, tumble out, tumble out, above and below, above and below.' He is in effect being accused of running his farm for profit to relieve his financial problems.*

The KING of BROBDINGNAG, and GULLIVER.

_Vide Swift's Gulliver: Voyage to Brobdingnag._

Pub.d June 26.th 1803. by H. Humphrey 27 S.t James's Street.

"My little friend Grildrig, you have made a most admirable "panegyric upon Yourself and Country, but from what I can "gather from your own relation & the answers I have with "much pains wringed & extorted from you, I cannot but con- -clude you to be, one of the most pernicious, little-odious- -reptiles, that nature ever suffer'd to crawl upon the surface of the Earth."

**The King of Brobdingnag, and Gulliver**

26 June 1803

JAMES GILLRAY

*This is a famous image published when Napoleon was preparing to invade England. George, as Jonathan Swift's King of Brobdingnag, in military uniform and a bag wig, dismisses the Gulliver Napoleon as 'one of the most pernicious, little – odious – reptiles, that nature ever suffer'd to crawl upon the surface of the Earth.' When George saw this print he commented, 'Quite wrong, quite wrong, no bag with uniform.'*

Prince Charles has contributed to the reassessment by focusing on the overlooked interests of George: his deep love of books, his active support of astronomy, his skill in architectural drawing and his fascination with mechanical instruments. He had a passionate love of music, which no other monarch of England has matched, and he did patronize the Arts, though usually at the instigation of other people. More recently, following the work of a new generation of historians on the creation of 'Britain' in the 18th century, George has emerged as the patriot king restraining his country from revolution and protecting it from the threat of military conquest.

In this book, I have tried to bring out the many facets of George's character. In the final analysis, the government of the country was the king's government and therefore he bears a considerable degree of responsibility for the policies chosen. He was unique among British monarchs in dismissing five Prime Ministers and he cannot be seen as the victim of political forces outside his control. He stiffened the stance of his weakest Prime Minister, who wanted some sort of settlement with the American colonies – their rebellion turned the King's natural conservatism into inflexible stubbornness. He tried hard to bring up his children in a loving and Christian way but the regime that he and his wife Charlotte imposed upon them inflicted untold misery.

At best, George had all the instincts of an English country squire: totally loyal to his friends; faithful to his wife; a lover of the countryside and farming; no trace of cowardice when faced with adversity; a belief in the decencies of life; and an overwhelming sense of patriotism. He loved his country and he saw it as his duty to bend all of his powers to cherish and protect it. Although George had few contacts with ordinary people, he had an affinity with them and he did his best to hold his country together in very turbulent times.

**God Save the King**

*This patriotic print with six illustrations of various verses from the national anthem was probably published for the King's golden jubilee in 1810. The black slaves in the main print rejoice at the ending of the British slave trade, which was outlawed in 1807, although slavery throughout the British Empire was not abolished until 1833. British ships are bringing wealth from India, Africa and the West Indies; life at home in Britain is protected by Britannia, with the cap of liberty atop her staff; and the Lion basks in peace before the castle and the cottage. George was the father of his people, the great survivor, whom at last the country had come to admire and cherish. Even God was on the side of Britain. It is probably the first illustrated version of the national anthem.*

# GOD SAVE THE KING.

save great George our King,    Long live our noble King,    God save the King.

O Lord our God arise,
Scatter his enemies,
And make them fall.
Confound their politicks,
Frustrate their Knavish tricks,

On George our hopes we fix,
God save us all.

Thy choicest gifts in store,
On him be pleas'd to pour,
Long may he reign.

May he defend our laws,
And ever give us cause,
With heart and voice to sing,
God save the King.

# 1 No Petticoat Government, No Scotch Minister

GEORGE, THE ELDEST SON of Frederick, Prince of Wales, and his wife, Princess Augusta of Saxe-Gotha, was born on 4 June 1738 in Norfolk House, St James's Square. George II and his wife could not stand the sight of their son Frederick, believing him to be 'the greatest villain ever born'. Frederick was small, ungainly, devious and reckless with money. Robert Walpole thought he was a 'poor, weak, irresolute, false, lying, dishonest, contemptible wretch that nobody loves, that nobody believes, that nobody will trust.' When he died in 1751 at the age of forty-four, George II bluntly declared, 'This has been a fatal year in my family. I lost my eldest son but was glad of it.' His twelve-year-old grandson George now became the Prince of Wales.

George's tutor, adviser and confidant was John Stuart, third Earl of Bute (1713–92), a descendant of the Scottish royal family. He had come to London after the Jacobite rising of 1745, joined Prince Frederick's circle at Leicester House and was made one of his Lords of the Bedchamber in 1750. However, Frederick did not have a huge regard for Bute's political skills, remarking that he 'would have made an excellent ambassador in some proud little Court where there is nothing to do'. George, however, came to look upon Bute as a surrogate father: 'I daily find what a treasure you are to me.'

Bute was responsible for inculcating into the young Prince of Wales the concept of a king above faction, politics without party. Those ideas came from *Letters on the Spirit of Patriotism and on The Idea of a Patriot King*, published by Henry, Viscount Bolingbroke in 1749, which called for a monarch to be virtuous, impartial and powerful enough to override party so as to govern in the interests of the whole nation. It was really a throwback to the Stuarts' concept of kingship. With Bute at his side, George came to realize that government was at bottom the King's responsibility. George I was perceived to have surrendered much of his authority to Walpole, and George II as having been dominated by the Whig hegemony of Walpole, Henry Pelham and the Duke of Newcastle; George III had no intention of being a monarch subject to the control of an oligarchy and merely playing a tame and minor role in the affairs of his nation.

Throughout his life George held fast to two deeply held and quite unmoveable convictions: first his personal responsibility as the king of all his people, which was a trust that had been divinely given to him; and secondly, his commitment to his coronation oath to maintain the rights and privileges of the Church of England, an obligation that overrode all other matters.

In 1751, Augusta was a widow of thirty-two and Bute was thirty-eight: he was handsome, with 'the best legs in London', red hair and an imposing presence, although reputedly happily married and a deeply religious man. Horace Walpole was quite convinced that the pair were lovers: 'The eagerness of the pages of the backstairs to let her know whenever Lord Bute arrived, a mellowness in her German accent as often as she spoke to him, and that was often, and a long, and a more than usual swimmingness in her eyes, contributed to dispel the ideas that had been conceived of the rigour of her widowhood.' Whatever the reality, and there is little evidence beyond gossip, it meant advancement for Bute: the Princess Dowager appointed him personal tutor to George in 1755 and the following year, on achieving his majority at eighteen, the Prince himself appointed Bute as Groom of the Stole. George Selwyn, the celebrated wit, said that Bute's nomination to the Privy Council on George's accession in 1760 was not due to faction but to 'fuction'. The satirists believed this – one print called her the Wanton Widow – and a broadside ballad, 'The Staff of Gisbal', began:

> When this notable chief of the Hebronites' land
> Before Bathsheba stood with his staff in his hand
> The damsels around her cried out one and all,
> 'What a wonderful…is the Staff of Gisbal!'

In 1761, George wrote to Bute: 'They have treated my Mother in a cruel manner (which I will never forget nor forgive till the day of my death).'

Bute was also responsible for stopping George marrying Lady Sarah Lennox, youngest daughter of the Duke of Richmond, and a great-granddaughter of Charles II. Six years younger than George, she was not yet fifteen when he saw her at Court and became infatuated; he considered her 'the most charming of her sex'. Though George pleaded with him 'to devise any method for keeping my love', he eventually accepted Bute's veto.

Bute's rise to power was unusual in that it was entirely dependent on personal favour, for he had little political

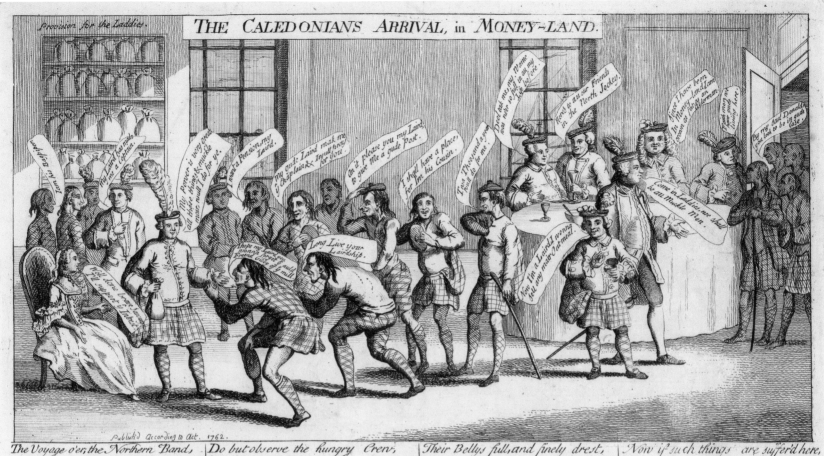

The Caledonians Arrival, in Money-Land

## The Caledonians Arrival, in Money-Land

May 1762

A group of ravenous Scots, some without breeches, have arrived in London – Money-Land – asking Bute for pensions, posts, chaplaincies, captaincies, and one even claims he has been appointed the official Bagpiper. Bute, now First Lord of the Treasury, supported by Augusta, Princess Dowager of Wales, hands out bags of money, of which there are many more on the shelf. The verses beneath the print spell out the danger to England:

> Their Bellys full, and finely drest,
> They shew themselves in all their best;
> While Englishmen are now turn'd out,
> To please ye Laddies of the Boot

There was anti-Scot sentiment throughout this period. The popular polemicist Junius, in his notorious letter to the King of 19 December 1769, saw a parallel between the Scots and the Jews: 'Like another chosen people, they have been conducted into the land of plenty, where they find themselves effectually marked, and divided from mankind.'

experience and had not held public office prior to his elevation when George became king. On hearing of his grandfather's death, the first letter George III sent was to Bute and within two days of his accession he had made him a member of his Privy Council. A fortnight later a paper was fixed on the Royal Exchange bearing the words, 'No petticoat government. No Scotch minister.' In May 1762, Bute was promoted Secretary of State for the North, the third most senior post in the government. Bute however had very few friends and his aloofness did not help. Shelburne, a leading Whig of the Pitt faction, described him as 'insolent and cowardly – rash and timid – had the perpetual apprehension of being governed – was always upon stilts – never natural except now and then upon the subject of women'.

George hoped that Bute would see-off the Whigs since his antipathy to them had grown by 1760 to unremitting hostility. The Whigs were the ruling party of England 1688–1760. They were an oligarchy – only 14 per cent of the male population had the vote – but in 1688 they had taken up arms to overthrow a Catholic king and to establish the sovereignty of Parliament. Having created the Protestant monarchy they preserved it principally under the premiership of Robert Walpole, but this was accompanied by religious toleration, freedom of speech and the supremacy of the rule of law.

The political system they had developed was unique in Europe and they believed that they had a natural right to be in charge of it. Yet in the seventy-seven years from 1760, the accession of George, to the death of his son William IV in 1837, the Whigs held power for only ten years, and all their administrations were uneasy coalitions which quickly fell apart. They were riven by factions formed around the great Whig families. They had no manifesto and they seemed to stand for nothing.

The Whigs were always more than a political party: they were a caste complete with their own traditions, family relationships and loyalties – all of which buttressed their natural position of being the governing class. Their leaders were grandees of immense wealth: the Duke of Devonshire owned so much of Derbyshire that he referred to it as 'my little kingdom'. The Dukes of Bedford owned vast tracts of Bedfordshire and Devon; the Marquis of Rockingham spent a fortune in Yorkshire building Wentworth Woodhouse, a palace that was grander than any owned by the King; and then there was the Earl of Leicester at Holkham Hall, and Lord Carlisle at Castle Howard. Their politics were conducted not at court but in their country palaces, in their splendid London houses, in their clubs and around their dining tables.

The government of Pitt the Elder and the Duke of Newcastle, which George inherited, soon fell apart over the conduct of the war and negotiations for a peace treaty. Under Bute's influence, George sought to end Britain's costly involvement in the Seven Years War. Pitt resigned in 1761 and Newcastle in 1762. Bute accepted the post of First Lord of the Treasury in May 1762 with great reluctance as he suffered from insomnia and had problems with his bowels. He did not want the job and he came to detest it. George insisted that he wanted a Prime Minister devoid of Newcastle's 'dirty arts' of patronage, but Bute had no political authority other than the King's favour. Edmund Burke in *Thoughts on the Cause of the Present Discontents* (1770) identified his weakness as lacking the only two securities: 'power arising from popularity; and power arising from connection.' Bute had neither. By the autumn he had to bring into his government the old Whig Henry Fox – the acknowledged expert in corrupt practices – whose task was to bribe MPs to vote for the peace treaty with France. In one morning £25,000 (nearly £1.8 million in today's money) was spent on bribery; and trafficking votes in Parliament became so open that members assembled outside the Paymaster's Office to receive their wages. George, who had wanted to stop corruption, had sadly to accept that 'we must call in bad men to govern bad men'.

Bute's rise to power in London and the control he had over offices raised a storm of protest from English politicians. He challenged the power of the Establishment which rested on the great English Whig families and was sustained by patronage – they were not going to give that up to a stranger from Scotland. On the very day that he resigned in April 1763 he made eighteen appointments, sixteen of which went to Scotsmen.

A media war broke out. William Hogarth, the greatest engraver of his generation, struck a blow for Bute in 1762 with his print, *The Times, Plate I*, which showed the Scots supporting a beleaguered king. However, the prints were overwhelmingly hostile to Bute. Among more than 400 caricatures that appeared over eighteen months, only four were favourable to Bute. A weekly paper which Bute financed, *The Briton*, deplored that 'the most indecent prints which obscenity and impudence can contrive were available to any passer-by in London', and it called for them to be prosecuted. In June 1762, Horace Walpole noted, 'The new administration begins tempestuously. My father [Sir Robert Walpole] was not more abused after twenty years than Lord Bute was in twenty days. Weekly papers swarm and like other swarms of insects, sting.'

## John Bull's House sett in Flames

2 September 1762

*St James's Palace, the home of George III and Queen Charlotte, is in flames, fanned by Bute. He is identified by bellows with a thistle on them, but shows he can 'blow a stronger blast other ways'. His advice has imperilled the Crown and even the shamelessly corrupt Henry Fox is fleeing. The constitutional heroes are the men dousing the fire, led by the elder Pitt who says, 'Poor Mr Bull, I PITT-Y you and I will endeavour to quench the flames.' He is supported by Newcastle in the long wig; the King's uncle, the Duke of Cumberland; and the poet, the Rev. Charles Churchill, a friend of John Wilkes and the*

*scourge of Hogarth, is in the centre of the print carrying* North Briton, *the name of Wilkes's anti-Bute weekly. The sign on the left being consumed by the flames carries the words, 'New Lost Land', a reference to the French capture of Newfoundland in June 1762.*

*This print implies that George is John Bull who is being led astray by his ministers and it has a particular significance since it provoked Hogarth to produce one of his very rare political prints – The Times, Plate I.*

IOHN BULL's HOUSE sett in FLAMES

Bute was enormously unpopular and when Parliament opened in November 1762 his bodyguard of boxers had to stop a mob attacking his sedan chair. However, thanks to Henry Fox's potent bribery he got parliamentary approval – by 319 votes to 65 – for his peace treaty with France, in spite of Pitt's eloquent three-and-a-half-hour denunciation. This victory was swiftly followed by the 'Massacre of the Pelhamite Innocents' a purge of Whig grandees. It seemed as if the worst was over. Augusta declared, 'Now my son is King of England.'

George rejected Bute's pleas to be relieved of office, but unable to stand it any longer he resigned in April 1763 – the victim of the first successful media campaign directed at a Prime Minister. Bute's influence waned. In 1766, George was tricked by Augusta into meeting with Bute, but when George told him he could not see him unless his ministers approved Bute angrily replied that he 'would never see the King again'. George rejoined, 'Then, my lord, be it so, and then from henceforth we never meet again.' That was the end of the relationship. The satirists, however, for several years depicted Bute lurking behind a curtain as a sinister shadow, the power behind the throne. He may not have been a physical presence, but his influence continued as he had shaped George's philosophy at an impressionable age. Once imbued with an opinion, George stuck to it.

It was a bad beginning but the relationship of George and Bute was due to their both being lonely figures who needed each other. Bute, in the circle of George's father, Frederick, Prince of Wales, had never attempted to establish a political position for himself by cosying-up to MPs or forging a close association with any of the Whig grandees. He spent his time educating the young heir, who by his very position was an isolated figure. Like all Hanoverian heirs, he had not been inducted into the business of kingship, for his grandfather, George II, did not let him see any state papers or discuss matters of state with him. In this solitary position it is understandable that he turned to his tutor as a friend who had no truck with the elite and who imbued in him a sense of duty about his kingship.

Another of his tutors, Lord Waldegrave, had earlier identified some personal characteristics that were to shape his life: he would seldom do wrong 'except when he mistakes wrong for right', and when this happens 'it will be difficult to undeceive because he is uncommonly indolent and has strong prejudices'.

Designed & Engraved by W Hogarth

Times

Plate I

Published as the Act Directs
Sep.r 7 1762

## The Times, Plate I

7 September 1762

WILLIAM HOGARTH

*This is the most important of the three political prints that Hogarth published. It is an outburst arising from his bitter quarrel with John Wilkes who had become the major critic of Bute and the King. George, atop the 'union' fire engine, is the state fireman quelling the fires arising from the Seven Years War, which are engulfing the globe and are fanned by Pitt, who is arrogantly standing on stilts. From the attic of the Temple Coffee House, Wilkes and Charles Churchill assail the King with water, and in the foreground a man with a wheelbarrow tries to trip up a Scotsman (Bute). By depicting George as a fireman, the preserver of his nation and representative of his people, dousing the ambition, pride and folly of his opponents, this print evokes Sir William Blackstone's description of the quality of kingship: 'the fountain of justice and the general conservator of the peace of the kingdom. He is not the spring, but the reservoir.' For George, it doesn't come better than this.*

23

**The State Quack**

September 1762

*This is the most blatant attack on Bute's alleged affair with Augusta. Bute as a quack doctor is offering to the crowds the services of his 'Union Squirt'. To add to the entertainment of Londoners she is on her back 'in full swing' on a tightrope, being penetrated by a long pole which has a jackboot on its end. Bute was often alluded to or represented by a boot, a play on his name. An English sailor is about to cudgel a Scotsman while another Scot greets a Frenchman, restoring the 'auld alliance'. This is a clear accusation of treason, as England and France were at war.*

**Tempora Mutantur**

October 1762

*Standing behind the blindfolded George is Folly holding a rattle with the word 'Peace'. Augusta, Princess Dowager of Wales, is presenting Bute to the King, as he was responsible for the negotiations then concluding in Paris to end the Seven Years War. This is a bitter attack upon the peace terms. Fame is placing a laurel on the head of Pitt, who was against the peace terms as he consoles a weeping Britannia, while Minerva points to the fleet, which has broken masts, folded sails and brooms displayed to show it was up for sale. The soldier's sword is padlocked, the lion is muzzled and the Gallic cock crows. The poem below says:*

> *Lives there a Briton can with*
> *Truth dispute*
> *Pitt's is the Laurel; Fames false*
> *Trumpet B——.*
> *Yet fav'rites thrive, by Merit not*
> *their own:*
> *What Pity Folly stands so near*
> *the Throne.*

*Behold* **Britannia**
*Her Tears to wipe,*
*See Pallas indicate*
*Tho' Envy's Snakes*
*Padlock'd that In*

# TEMPORA MUTANTUR.—

and Pitt implore
piness restore;
triot's Fame,
he glorious Aim;
dreaded by our Foes

While Gallia's Cock aloud triumphant Crows:
Is this a Scene for Britons, bold and free,
Victors on Land, and Monarch's of the Sea?
Perhaps 'tis just—Heav'n meant it for our Crimes
Success must change whenever change the Times.

Lives there a Briton can with Truth dispute
Pitt's is the Laurel; Fames false Trumpet B—
Yet fav'rites thrive, by Merit not their own:
What Pity Folly stands so near the Throne.

## Excise – Resignation

8 April 1763

On 8 April, Bute together with the Chancellor of the Exchequer, Sir Francis Dashwood, and Henry Fox, the Leader of the Commons, resigned. In his youth, Dashwood had been the founder of the notorious Hell-Fire Club and his appointment as Chancellor had evoked the jibe from Wilkes that he had been 'puzzling all his life over tavern bills'. In March 1763, faced with a National Debt that had doubled during the war, he proposed a tax on cider – 4 shillings on each hogshead – which would come within the jurisdication of the hated Excise, and all for just the footling revenue of £75,000 (£5.4 million). The fate of Bute's government was sealed. MPs representing the apple-growing regions of Devon, Somerset, Warwickshire, Gloucestershire and

# RESIGNATION

*Well said Unde drive him to the Gallows*

*Never fear Ned he's true Preston Bred*

*O spare my Monhood, and I'se gang quietly.*

*I'll soon spoil your Piping Iwarrant you*

*O what pain it is to part Can thy P leave thee.*

RE.
his due:
al prints Call'd
TION.
larly continued every
tire Tavern

*Fam'd Albion's Sons behold a Sight,*
*Must give each loyal Heart delight*
*He who your Magna Charta Sold,*
*Old Nick at last has got in hold*
*And Swears he'll send him with all speed*
*Acrass the Styx instead of Tweed,*
*While Madam's Tears too plainly tell*
*She mourns his loss who Pip'd so well.*

Herefordshire rose up in their wrath and howled Bute down when he argued that as beer was taxed, why not cider? Here farmers welcome his hanging and also that of Fox, around whose neck hang moneybags: as Paymaster General during the Seven Years War he had accumulated a personal fortune, a peculation that had been attacked in the Commons in March.

In the accompanying print a very décolleté Augusta weeps at the departure of her lover, whose testicles have been grasped so painfully by a devil that Bute pleads, 'O spare my Monhood, and I'se gang quietly.' This happy scene is watched by a goat, the symbol of rampant sexuality, which makes an obscene gesture towards the fallen Prime Minister. The closing line of verse says that Augusta 'mourns his loss who Pip'd so well'.

Claudius pouring Poison into the King's Ear, as he is Sleeping in the Garden. — Scene in Hamlet Act I. Scene III.

## Claudius pouring Poison into the King's Ear, as he is Sleeping in the Garden

February 1769

OXFORD MAGAZINE

*Bute, who used to appear in amateur theatricals at Leicester House, the home of Frederick, Prince of Wales, when George was young, here plays Claudius in* Hamlet. *Together with Augusta, the Princess Dowager of Wales, as Gertrude, he pours poison into the sleeping king's ear. In Charles Churchill's words, they are 'poisoning the royal ear of power'. The satirists, six years after Bute's resignation, still believed that he was the power behind the throne. In fact, since 1766 Bute had been excluded from the advisers around George III and from 1769, when this print appeared, to 1771 he was travelling in Italy.*

The RECEPTION in 1760.

The Reception in 1770 in our next.

The RECEPTION in 1770.

**The Reception in 1760**

March 1770

*OXFORD MAGAZINE*

**The Reception in 1770**

April 1770

*OXFORD MAGAZINE*

*This is the sharp contrast between the popularity of the King on his accession – cheering crowds waving from the windows, 'Honour & Glory to the British King' – and the coolness of his reception in 1770. Grafton, First Lord of the Treasury, drives a coach dressed as a jockey, and the Yeoman of the Guard in the centre has become a Scot. The* Oxford Magazine, *in its commentary on the print, made him speak in the Scottish dialect: 'Your Majesty mun ken that ya ba not attended noo by tha scoom of the yerth.'*

## 2 **The Rake on the Make**

WHEN BUTE RESIGNED George had a real problem finding a successor. Fox was too corrupt, Newcastle too old, Shelburne too young, Bedford too lazy, and so by default he turned to Pitt's brother-in-law George Grenville, whose ability he had earlier described as 'unfit for a post where either decision or activity are necessary'. Grenville was in fact conscientious and hard-working by the standards of the time, though rather pompous and stubborn, and had a good deal of parliamentary experience. However, he made two great mistakes. He used the power of Parliament to attack John Wilkes and the power of the Treasury to tax the American colonies, and in both of these he had the enthusiastic support of George.

Wilkes was MP for Aylesbury and lived by his wits. Boss-eyed, a polemical journalist, an embezzler of charitable funds,

### John Wilkes Esqr.

16 May 1763

WILLIAM HOGARTH

*On 6 May 1763 Wilkes has been brought from the Tower of London, where he had been held under a general warrant from 29 April, to a hearing in Westminster Hall before Chief Justice Pratt. Pratt decided that Wilkes should go free – a judgment received with cheers and cries of 'Wilkes and Liberty'. Hogarth was present, and in the words of Charles Churchill, the satirical poet and Wilkes's friend, he was:*

> *Lurking, most ruffian-like, behind a screen*
> *So plac'd all things to see, himself unseen,*
> *Virtue, with due contempt, saw Hogarth stand,*
> *The murd'rous pencil in his palsied hand.*

*The antipathy between the two had started the previous autumn. Hogarth's official post of Serjeant-Painter to the King depended upon the favour of Bute and the King and in* The Times, Plate 1 *(see pp. 22–23) he gave a favourable view of George saving the nation from the ambitions of Pitt. Wilkes responded by devoting the entire edition of the* North Briton *of 25 September to an attack upon Hogarth for his defence of the government. Hogarth's revenge was this devastating portrait. His biographer Jenny Uglow describes the 'jesting arrogance and sexy defiance of Wilkes....His squint is just slightly exaggerated to turn his grin into the leer of a cynic; his wig is just slightly curled back into the horns of a devil. He twirls the cap of liberty on its pole, a laughing man who would exploit the very people he seduced.' Poor Wilkes, skewered for eternity.*

*John Wilkes Esqr.*
Drawn from the Life and Etch'd in Aquafortis by Wil.m Hogarth.
Price 1 Shilling.    Publish'd according to Act of Parliament . May 4 16 1763.

## Kaw, Jack, have Canada or to the Tower

April 1763

*Wilkes launched the* North Briton *in June 1762. Appearing each Saturday, it soon acquired a strong following for its acerbic attacks on Bute, Henry Fox and the Scots. Issue No. 23 openly condemned Fox, Paymaster General, for 'his breaches of private faith and his abuses of public trust....The greatness of his understanding serves only to make the badness of his heart more formidable.' Subtle and devious, Fox did not sue for libel but instead is alleged to have tried to buy off his bitterest critic by offering him the governorship of Canada. In this print Bute, with a devil's tail and wings and the Scottish imps Temora and Fingal climbing his shoulder, is offering both a monetary bribe to Wilkes and a stick with the choice of Canada or the Tower:*

> *The empire of Canada lyes at your feet,*
> *To plunder and fleece – what a delicate treat.*

*Wilkes turned it down:*

> *Avaunt, vile corrupter, I'll take no such thing,*
> *I'll be true to old England, the Whigs, and the King!*

*Behind Wilkes is one of his supporters, the Whig grandee Lord Temple, brother-in-law of Pitt the Elder.*

an English nationalist with a good eye for turning a political situation to his advantage, a member of the Hell-Fire Club and a libertine who kept condoms in an envelope in his desk – he was the rake on the make. He disliked the way in which the new king, George III, was using his powers, but above all he disliked having a Scotsman, Lord Bute, as first minister of England. He decided to strike at both of them. In 1762, within a week of Bute establishing *The Briton* under the editorship of Tobias Smollett to further government policies, Wilkes published the *North Briton*. Its aim was to attack Bute by playing upon traditional prejudice against the Scots and in its very title alluded to Bute and Smollett's Scottish origins.

Issue No. 45 of the *North Briton* in April 1763 became a *cause célèbre* that made Wilkes a household name. It described George III's speech to Parliament, which commended Bute's Treaty of Paris ending the Seven Years War, as 'the most abandoned instance of ministerial effrontery ever attempted to be imposed upon mankind'. The honour of the Crown was 'sunk even to prostitution'. A general warrant was issued for the arrest of 'the authors, printers and publishers of the *North Briton*, No. 45' on a charge of libel. Wilkes was thrown into the Tower of London, but a fortnight later Chief Justice Pratt in the Court of Common Pleas, a member of the Chatham faction, released him on the grounds that an MP was privileged against arrest for libel. Wilkes somewhat surprisingly became the champion of the old historic rights of England. The cry 'Wilkes and Liberty!' was taken up by the London mob and was to echo around the country to the torment of George III.

While he was in the Tower, Wilkes had cheekily sued Lord Halifax, the Secretary of State, who had issued the general warrant. Fortunately for Wilkes, his case once again came before Chief Justice Pratt, who delivered the famous judgment that general warrants were illegal; that reasons of state were not pleadable in English courts; and that the Secretary of State was as answerable as any other man for his actions. It was a great step for liberty; if Wilkes had come up before Lord Mansfield of the Court of King's Bench, a supporter of the government, the outcome might have been very different.

Wilkes did not have it all his own way, however. Hogarth, who had a grudge against him, produced his famous caricature, saying he did it to 'stop a gap in my income'. Moreover, Wilkes had shared in the writing of an obscene and occasionally blasphemous poem, *An Essay on Woman*, a parody of Pope's *Essay on Man*, to be circulated among friends. Wilkes did not hide his randiness, confiding to Boswell, 'I wrote my best *North Briton* in bed with Betsy Green.' He set up a press in his house to do a reprint of the *North Briton* and also printed part of the poem. Lord Sandwich, one of Grenville's ministers, master-minded a scheme to get hold of some proofs, eventually by bribing one of Wilkes's printers. In November 1763, the profligate Sandwich, a fellow member of the Hell-Fire Club and an erstwhile friend of Wilkes, rose in the Lords to condemn the *Essay* and quoted shocking passages – on the same day that the Commons was debating, at the King's insistence, a motion that declared No. 45 scandalous and seditious. In December, Wilkes fled to France and spent most of the next four years there. In January 1764, the Commons voted to expel him and a writ was then issued for his arrest. George III believed that he had won.

Grenville's government became bogged down in trying to silence Wilkes and with the much wider issue of general warrants. Action was even taken against Wilkes while he was in exile. But Wilkes was popular – the spokesman for the ancient liberties of England which were the special possession of the Whigs – and he had the most eloquent speaker in the country, Pitt, as his champion. The King had been the first to demand that Grenville should lay the charge of libel and he was convinced that Wilkes – 'a rascal', an 'audacious character', 'that devil' – was an enemy of the state who had to be dealt with. Grenville knew that George's determination to suppress Wilkes was a personal matter – he hated him. But George was incapable

of seeing that the persecution of Wilkes was self-defeating. He was committed to the task of breaking the rake and all the unpopularity that that entailed – a wiser man would have cut his losses. In December 1763, Horace Walpole recorded that, 'The last time the King was at Drury Lane, the play given out for the next night was "All in the Wrong": the galleries clapped and then cried out, "Let us all be in the right! Wilkes and Liberty!" When the King comes to a theatre, or goes out or goes to the House, there is not a single applause.'

By 1765, however, George had tired of Grenville and particularly of his insistent and verbose demands for favours for his supporters: 'No office fell vacant in any department that Mr G did not declare he would not serve if the man he recommended did not succeed.' This coolness became even colder by Grenville's mishandling of a Regency Bill following George's first serious illness. George had had enough and he was not prepared 'to see the Crown dictated to by low men'. In July, he sacked Grenville and appointed the 35-year-old Marquis of Rockingham to be his Prime Minister. Rockingham was a poor speaker in the Lords, devoid of administrative or real political experience, cursed by ill-health and his only qualification for the high office was his personal charm.

Charles Townshend, a charismatic parliamentarian, described the government as 'a mere lutestring administration, pretty summer wear but it will never stand the winter'. He was right.

Engraved for the Oxford Magazine.

Hieroglyphics.

### Hieroglyphics

March 1769

OXFORD MAGAZINE

*Wilkes is savaged by two bloodhounds: on the right, the Prime Minister, the Duke of Grafton, and on the left, Sir Fletcher Norton, an MP and former Attorney General who was one of those attacking Wilkes.*
*The election of Wilkes for the seat of Middlesex was rendered void for the first time by a vote in the House of Commons on 3 February 1769, as Horace Walpole recorded: 'At past two in the morning the House divided; the courtiers were 239, the minority 135.'*
*By calling Wilkes's persecutors 'the courtiers', Walpole was clearly showing the King's personal involvement. Wilkes was re-elected and expelled again later in February and March. Wilkes shrewdly says his assailants can tear him to pieces, 'but spare, oh spare my bleeding Country'. He knew how to spin the news.*

At the start of his reign George had hoped to find men who would rise above faction so that government did not rely on the overweening power of the Whig grandees, but by 1766 it was business as usual – Robert Walpole would have been quite at home. George was only too glad to receive the advice from a disloyal Lord Chancellor, Northington, that the government could not continue, which he saw as an affirmation of his 'contempt for their talents'. On 9 July 1766, he dismissed Rockingham and appointed the man he most wanted, William Pitt, who was transformed from 'the blackest of hearts' to the 'dear friend'. He had been told that Pitt, 'the Great Commoner', had modified his anti-monarchical views; would not insist on conditions as he had done previously; and was willing to serve. At a stroke George was popular: the City of London loved the appointment and arranged a large fireworks party. But the whole political world was astonished that 'the Great Commoner' demanded a seat in the House of Lords as the Earl of Chatham. Lord Chesterfield was puzzled that Pitt was 'to withdraw in the fullness of power…from the House of Commons and to go into

## The Button Maker

April 1770

OXFORD MAGAZINE

*The King's fondness for turning buttons on a lathe had become public knowledge and was the subject of much satire. A mock petition in the* Oxford Magazine *from the 'Button-makers and journeymen' bewailed impending unemployment if their King went any further. The print implies that he spent more time making buttons – encouraged by obsequious courtiers – than listening to the arguments in a Remonstrance from the City of London which condemned the Commons for expelling Wilkes. On receiving it, the King had 'instantly turned round to his courtiers and burst out laughing'. Another costly mistake in his war with Wilkes occurred as Chatham moved a resolution against the government in the House of Lords, and the City Corporation drew up a third petition to present to George at St James's Palace. This too was rejected and on that occasion the Lord Mayor, William Beckford, an ally of Chatham's, stood his ground and, to everyone's amazement, answered back with a speech to the King that was subsequently printed in the press to much acclaim.*

*The Button Maker.*

**Advice to a Great K—g**

1770

*OXFORD MAGAZINE*

*George III is reading a pamphlet,* The False Alarm, *written by Dr Johnson in defence of the government's determination to exclude Wilkes. But on the table is a copy of the* Public Advertiser, *the newspaper that printed Junius's scathing attacks on the King and his ministers. The pictures on the wall,* The Patriot King *and* The Tyrant King, *and the advisers – one an angel and the other a devilish hag – tell George to abjure*

that Hospital of Incurables, the House of Lords'. Blunter critics dubbed him 'Lord Cheat-em' and the fireworks were cancelled. George had in fact chosen a man who was more unstable than himself. Depression bordering on madness took hold and Pitt left London, begging to be discharged, but George stubbornly refused.

This 'mosaic administration', in Burke's words, drove the Rockingham, Bedford and Grenville factions into opposition and Pitt became a mere figurehead. The Government descended into chaos. It was left in the hands of Charles Townshend, famous for his 'champagne speeches', but he died suddenly at the age of forty-two in September 1767, and the Duke of Grafton in effect became Prime Minister. Junius, the anonymous author of a series of mordant attacks on George's ministers, described Grafton as a 'young nobleman already ruined by play'. He was distracted by women and horses, and offended London society by flaunting his mistress, Nancy Parsons, on public occasions.

Wilkes, knowing that the government was in a mess, decided to stand as a candidate in the 1768 general election. His second appearance was to prove as disastrous for Grafton as his first appearance had been for Grenville. Although still outlawed, he returned from France and stood for the City of London constituency, but coming bottom of the poll he transferred to Middlesex, where he was elected. Wilkes then surrendered himself to the authorities and was committed to King's Bench prison, Southwark. It was not an arduous regime as he could pay fees to have a comfortable room. He continued to write letters and pamphlets, as well as receive the favours of several women. On 10 May 1768, there were riots outside the prison and seven people were killed by the King's soldiers: the St George's Fields Massacre. The Commons expelled him as the Member for Middlesex but he was quickly re-elected despite still being in prison. Then he was expelled from the House on

*personal government. Junius was more explicit in his notorious letter of December 1769: the House of Hanover could only survive if it totally renounced the ways of the House of Stuart: 'The prince who imitates their conduct, should be warned by their example; and while he plumes himself upon the security of his title to the crown, should remember that, as it was acquired by one revolution, it may be lost by another.'*

3 February 1769, re-elected on 16 February and re-elected yet again in March. George strongly urged the repeated expulsions as 'a measure whereupon my Crown almost depends'. He collected lists of MPs whose votes were for Wilkes.

Colonel Luttrell was persuaded to give up his Cornish seat to stand against Wilkes in a fourth election at Middlesex but was defeated – Wilkes received four times as many votes: 1,143 to Luttrell's 296. Church bells were rung. It would have been much better to have left Wilkes alone at that point but the government, goaded by the King, decided that an example had to be made. The Commons resolved by 197 to 143 votes that Luttrell 'ought to have been returned' as the MP for Middlesex. This provoked petitions from English counties condemning the corruption of Parliament and led to protests by large and often riotous crowds; the cry was heard, 'Wilkes and no King'. The Wilkes affair rumbled on but slowly faded; in 1774 he was elected MP for Middlesex for a fifth time but was now allowed to take his seat and remained in Parliament for sixteen years.

Nonetheless, the whole Wilkes controversy and the general conduct of government provoked a vitriolic attack on George by Junius in December 1769. The opening words of his notorious *Letter 35* addressed to the King were explosive: 'It is the misfortune of your life…that you should never have been acquainted with the language of truth, until you heard it in the complaints of your people.' Horace Walpole thought it was 'the most daring insult ever offered to a prince but in times of open rebellion'. Junius went on to condemn George's personal involvement in the persecution of Wilkes: 'Discard those little, personal resentments, which have too long directed your public conduct.'

In January 1770, Chatham launched an attack on the government and the damaging effect of the Wilkes affair was laid bare when Lord Camden (the former Chief Justice Pratt), now Lord Chancellor, supported a motion of censure on his own government over the Luttrell-Wilkes election. He spoke of its 'arbitrary measures' which for some time had meant that he had 'dropped and hung his head in Council'. Grafton's government disintegrated under the pressure and he resigned. George III was not prepared to consider either Rockingham or Chatham; his new rock would be Lord North, who became First Lord of the Treasury on 31 January 1770.

## The Parricide

1 May 1776

*WESTMINSTER MAGAZINE*

*This is a rare attack on opponents of George's American policy. It accuses them of helping America to destroy Britain. Anger is directed against the so-called 'patriots': Chatham; Fox; Grafton, who is actually restraining Britannia's arm; Camden, who is muzzling the lion; and Wilkes, directing the dagger of the woman with an Indian headdress towards Britannia's heart. In America, Wilkes had become a hero in liberty-loving circles for standing up to the arbitrary power of the King. The number 45, from the famed issue No. 45 of the North Briton, was worn by some patriots on their caps; on the 45th day of 1770, 45 New York citizens ate 45 pounds of beefsteak from a bullock 45 months old.*

*The Parricide.*
*A Sketch of Modern Patriotism.*

# 3 The Blind Trumpeter, 1770–1782

FREDERICK, LORD NORTH, had started his public life in 1754 when, at the age of twenty-two, he took the family seat of Banbury in the House of Commons. His dry humour and affability made him popular in the Commons. After holding a junior office in the Treasury, he was appointed in 1767 by Grafton as Chancellor of the Exchequer, a post he was to hold for fifteen years, combining it with the premiership from 1770 to 1782.

For ten years George had searched for a prime minister who could rise above the competing factions in the great battle of Westminster politics. After Bute he had had to turn again to the Whigs and had three successive first ministers – Grenville, Rockingham and Grafton – all of whom were dismissed as they could not establish an effective working relationship with him. In appointing North as the First Lord of the Treasury George seemed to have found, at last, a congenial and competent Tory. North was a shrewd parliamentary tactician, a popular MP and a successful Chancellor of the Exchequer, but he was also soft and pliable. North needed guidance just as much as George wanted a chief minister who was a friend to confide in and who would respond sympathetically to his views. It proved to be one of the most disastrous political partnerships in British history.

*Engrav'd for the Oxford Magazine.*

*Remarkable Characters at M.<sup>rs</sup> Cornellys Masquerade.*

There was a remarkable complementarity in their relationship. On major issues – notably American taxation – they thought alike, buttressing each other's prejudices and reinforcing a common stubbornness. George wanted a sympathetic and compliant Prime Minister, someone who would work with the grain of his own attitudes and instincts, and who had an instinctive reverence for the role of the monarchy. North, for his part, having spent his youth under the domination of a very strong father, appeared content to succumb to a more forceful partner and this relationship seemed to meet a need in his nature. Many attested to his kindness, decency and good humour but he was naturally indolent and although this conveyed a reassuring imperturbability it was not the quality that was needed to deal with the political crises which were about to engulf the nation. He was a soft plump man, often portrayed as half-asleep and with an absence of vigour.

## Remarkable Characters at Mrs Cornellys Masquerade

March 1770

OXFORD MAGAZINE

*Originally an opera singer in Venice, Mrs Teresa Cornelys was quite a girl, being the first paramour of Casanova. For two decades after her arrival in London in 1759 she gave the smartest and most fashionable parties at Carlisle House in Soho and they attracted a lot of press attention – the paparazzi would have been out in force on 26 February 1770. The King would certainly not have attended. In this print he is shown wearing the clothes of a child and bearing a rattle. He does not like the image that the satyr holds up to him; he is still under the control of Bute, who holds his reins. Fletcher Norton, the noted lawyer, often ridiculed as 'Sir Bullface Doublefee', and recently elected Speaker of the House of Commons, is depicted as a devil. But at least he recognizes, as does Bute, that a new wind is blowing from North, who had become Prime Minister at the end of January. The party is going on while London burns. Mrs Cornelys died miserably poor in the Fleet Prison in 1797.*

Engrav'd for the Oxford Magazine.

Nero Fiddling, Rome Burning, Pompaja & Agrippina Smiling

## Nero Fiddling, Rome Burning, Pompaja & Agrippina Smiling

May 1770

OXFORD MAGAZINE

*This cartoon marks the shift from depicting George as a fool to depicting him as a knave. Urged on by Pompaja (Queen Charlotte) and by Agrippina (his mother the Princess Dowager of Wales) George tramples on the* Laws of Humanity *and the* Laws of Discretion, *and plays the fiddle while London burns: 'What a Charming Blaze! This shall make them know I am their Master.'*

## The Young Heir among bad Councellors, or the Lion betray'd

1 June 1771

*OXFORD MAGAZINE*

*Several prints in 1770 and 1771 portray George blindfolded – the victim of his ministers. Sandwich is on the left; North's cloven leg stabs the lion's breast; and Grafton, Mansfield and the Speaker, Fletcher 'Sir Bullface Doublefee' Norton, all offer their services. The text of a letter accompanying this print blames Bute for George's ingratitude to the Whigs: 'Sir, I knew a young gentleman, who when he first became possessed of a large estate, was idolized and adored by the tenants of his grandfather, from whom he inherited; but, unhappily for him, he suffered himself to be swayed by a north country servant, who led him into all manner of errors. The first article that was recommended to his practice was ingratitude; and the descendants of those, whose ancestors brought the family of this young man into the actual possession of the estate he now enjoys, at the hazard of their lives and fortunes, are now discarded with contempt.'*

The Young Heir among bad Councellors, or the Lion betray'd.

*I Promise to reduce the Americans.*

## Boreas – The Blind Trumpeter

September 1774

OXFORD MAGAZINE

Boreas was the Greek god of the North wind. This caricature appeared just before a general election, when North made a pledge, 'I Promise to reduce the Americans', that proved to be disastrous. Horace Walpole described North in his Memoirs:

'Nothing could be more coarse or clumsy or ungracious than his outside. Two large prominent eyes that rolled about to no purpose (for he was utterly short-sighted), a wide mouth, thick lips and inflated visage, gave him the air of a blind trumpeter. A deep untuneful voice which, instead of modulating, he enforced with unnecessary pomp, a total neglect of his person, and ignorance of every civil attention, disgusted all who judge by appearance, or without their approbation until it is courted. But within that rude casket were enclosed many useful talents. He had much wit, strong natural sense, assurance and promptness. What he did, he did without a mask, and was not delicate in choosing his means.'

## The Colossus of the North; or The Striding Boreas

1 December 1774

LONDON MAGAZINE

North was at the height of his powers. He called a snap election in the autumn of 1774 and was returned with a slightly increased majority. Yet the means are clear: he straddles a stream of MPs who by bribery and corruption have carried him to victory; he stands on Tyranny and Venality and he flourishes Pensions, Places and Lottery Tickets. North told the Treasury Secretary to agree to pay Lord Falmouth £2,500 for each of the six seats he controlled, and was offended when Lord Edgcumbe wanted £3,000 for each of his five. Wilkes, recently elected Lord Mayor of London, boasts to Britannia that he will stem the stream, but Nemesis, in the shape of the flaming torch America, is about to strike.

*The Colossus of the North; or The Striding Boreas.*

*See our Colossus strides with Trophies crown'd,*
*And Monsters in Corruption's Stream abound.*

*The Political Cartoon, for the Year 1775.*

**The Political Cartoon, for the Year 1775**

1 May 1775

*WESTMINSTER MAGAZINE*

*George's two-wheeled chaise, drawn by the horses Obstinacy and Pride and driven by the Chief Justice Lord Mansfield, is about to plunge into a great abyss. Bute, as the groom, is seen as the dispenser of pensions (which he no longer was) and Chatham, on crutches, gesticulates in despair. Magna Carta is crushed by the wheels of the chaise. A government minister in the foreground bribes the people and the Scots on the left count their profits. The National Credit is carried away by a devil. George is either asleep or blind; in either case he is oblivious to the fires that are raging in the distance in America. The King's popularity at the start of his reign has evaporated – he is seen to be the driving force behind his failed ministers and it is he who is betraying the national interest.*

Over the years North has had a bad press and certainly has a high place in the list of Britain's worst Prime Ministers. But all his virtuous qualities – an easy temperament, loyalty to his friends and devotion to his wife and family – cannot excuse the fact that he was a political failure who presided over a massive national humiliation. He did not have the imaginative capacity of Chatham, who realized that Britain could not subdue America, nor did he have the ability to formulate and carry through new policies suited to the problems. The first four years of North's administration were relatively quiet due to his masterly handling of the Commons – he was by nature a chief whip – which secured steady majorities for the government's measures. However, America had already started to intrude into and

### Grace before Meat or a Peep at Lord Peter's

1778

JAMES GILLRAY

*In 1778, at the height of the American War, George and Charlotte were entertained by the Catholic Lord Petre at his house in Essex when they were visiting Warley Camp. The modest provisions of the Catholic Relief Act of that year were strongly opposed by Protestant groups across the country; this 'No Popery' attack on George was intended as a warning that no further concessions should be made. This is the first print attributed to Gillray and therefore his first depiction of George III and Queen Charlotte.*

GRACE BEFORE MEAT or a Peep at Lord PETER'S.

subsequently to dominate British politics. (The American Revolution is covered in the next chapter.)

In all his measures North had the full support of the King but his government was soon overwhelmed with the crisis in the American colonies. At the heart of the conflict was the question of authority. The Crown through Parliament had the absolute right to govern the American colonies just as they governed the English counties. London could levy taxes, control trade and appoint governors to run their colonies with no democratic involvement of the colonists. If that was challenged then the very authority of the Crown in Parliament was challenged. Both George and North could not believe that a bunch of colonial farmers with no army, little tradition of democratic government, no antipathy to institutionalized smuggling and no scruple about using violence against London's decisions, could be allowed to govern themselves. All of this confirmed George's view that the Americans were 'an unhappy, misled, deluded multitude'.

An aggravating factor throughout the 1770s was that the King was actively engaged in the great and small issues of state. Neither his temperament nor his sense of duty allowed him to relax – his finger was in every pie and his voluminous letters reveal his constant involvement in the decisions of government. He started as early as 1761 in micro-managing his household by setting the wages and privileges of the royal laundresses. He summoned a cabinet minister to explain to him the design of ships; he proposed to the Cabinet how recruits should be raised across the country for the army; he advised North on the timing of parliamentary business to take advantage of Charles James Fox's absence overseas; he insisted in 1781 that North appoint a bishop to the see of Winchester even before the incumbent had died; he decided which admiral should command a squadron and how many ships should sail to the West Indies; and he warned North not to promise offices without consulting him. His ministers could be assured that he had a view on everything. He told Lord Sandwich, First Lord of the Admiralty, that 'if others will not be active, I must drive'. George was a control freak.

After Burgoyne and his army had been forced to capitulate at Saratoga in 1777, North realized that he was not a competent war leader and he was quite prepared to reach a compromise settlement with the American rebels on any terms short of actual independence. But it was too late – the famous declaration had been issued in 1776. In a series of letters he begged George to release him from office and proposed Chatham as a replacement. They are rather pathetic in their frankness but one cannot help feeling some sympathy for a man who was stretched beyond his natural abilities. George mercilessly bullied North: 'Are you resolved, agreeable to the example of the Duke of Grafton, at the hour of danger, to desert me?' George would not let him go. Lashed together like Captain Ahab on the great whale Moby Dick, they plunged together to the depths.

The many favours North received from the King helped to cement their relationship: 'I'm under such obligations to the King, that I can never leave his service while he desires me to remain in it.' He became a Knight of the Garter and George helped him financially, for North was not a rich man and he had several children to support. George provided £20,000 (£1.4 million in today's money) to pay off his debts and in 1778 appointed him Lord Warden of the Cinque Ports, which was worth £4,000 (£280,000) a year.

### The Botching Taylor Cutting his Cloth to cover a Button

27 December 1779

JOHN SIMPSON

*This is an attack upon the misgovernment of North's administration which had led to dissatisfaction and disgrace. It is a gathering of the guilty and even Bute is included, though at this time he had no influence. North mournfully holds a bolt of cloth bearing the names 'America', 'West Indies' and 'Africa', while the King's cloth names 'Ireland', 'Great Britain' and 'Hanover'. Between them they are trampling on old historic rights and making a mess of their national and international responsibilities. The King is the most to blame and is ridiculed for his button-making: a broadside hanging on the wall is 'The Button-makers Downfall or Ruin to Old England to the tune of Britons strike Home'.*

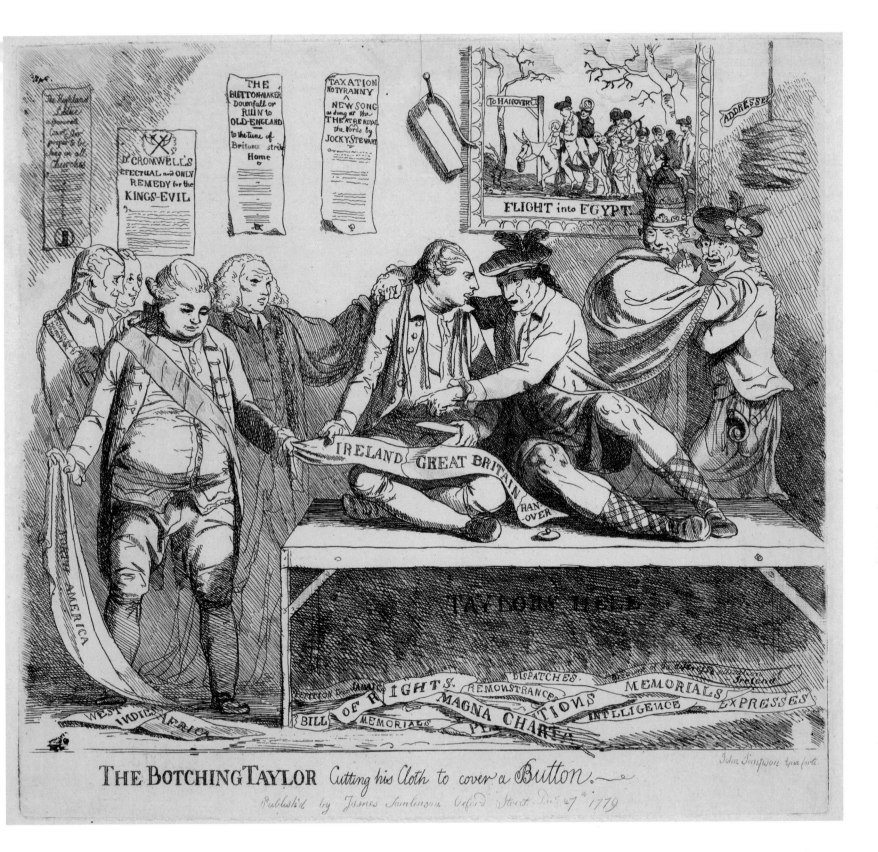

THE BLIND TRUMPETER, 1770–1782 **43**

## The State Tinkers

10 February 1780

JAMES GILLRAY

*The verse at the bottom of this print clearly attributes the state of the nation to George, who is watching North chip away at the inside of the National Kettle – the Constitution – while Sandwich, First Lord of the Admiralty, and Lord George Germain, Secretary of State for America, hammer holes into it from the outside. George's crown rests on a turban, implying oriental despotism. Gillray hints at much more, as tinkers since the 17th century had been seen as a dangerous underclass threatening the stability of the nation and here it is George's very ministers who are playing that part. The verse reads:*

*The National Kettle, which once
was a good one,
For boiling of Mutton, of Beef, &
of Pudding,
By the fault of the Cook, was
quite out of repair,
When the Tinkers were sent for, –
Behold them & Stare.*

*The Master he thinks, they are
wonderful Clever,
And cries out in raptures, 'tis
done! now or never!
Yet sneering the Tinkers their old
Trade pursue,
In stopping of one Hole – they're
sure to make Two.*

## THE STATE TINKERS.

The National Kettle, which once was a good one,
For boiling of Mutton, of Beef, & of Pudding,
By the fault of the Cook, was quite out of repair,
When the Tinkers were sent for, ___ Behold them & Stare.

The Master he thinks, they are wonderful Clever, ___
And cries out in raptures, 'tis done! now or never!
Yet sneering the Tinkers their old Trade pursue, ___
In stopping of one Hole ___ they're sure to make Two.

Publish'd Feb.ʳ 10ᵗʰ 1780 by W. Humphrey N.º 227 Strand.

## Prerogatives Defeat or Liberties Triumph

20 April 1780

*John Dunning, a Whig MP, moved on 6 April his famous motion 'That the influence of the Crown has increased, is increasing, and ought to be diminished.' It was carried by 233 votes to 215. Here Dunning tramples on Bute and North while Charles James Fox welcomes him warmly with the words, 'Influence is the Masked Battery of Tyranny.' A Native American and an Irish Volunteer relish this attack upon their sovereign. The Native American says, 'Now we will treat with them' and the Volunteer: 'We are Loyal but we will be Free.' North's government lasted a further two years but this was the beginning of the end.*

PREROGATIVES DEFEAT or LIBERTIES TRIUMPH

## Ecclesiastical and Political state of the Nation

2 June 1780

JAMES GILLRAY (?)

*In the early months of 1780 the government was on the defensive: Edmund Burke launched a series of scathing attacks over public expenditure; county committees were demanding an end to corruption; the Protestant Associations of England and Scotland, whipped up by their leader Lord George Gordon, flooded the House with petitions for the repeal of the Catholic Relief Act of 1778; and on 6 April Dunning's famous motion criticising the influence of the Crown was passed.*

*This print, a piece of 'No Popery' propaganda, accuses the King of being so blind to what is happening that he ploughs the land for Jesuits and Catholics to sow their seeds. North drives the bull to safe Protestant Scotland, abandoning his duty, and the Church of England in the shape of a bishop is fast asleep in the foreground. The extreme Protestants believed that the King had been taken in by the Catholics and had betrayed his coronation oath.*

*The publication of the print was timed to coincide with a huge meeting on 2 June of the Protestant Association in St George's Fields, Southwark, which marched on Westminster to present a big petition for the repeal of the Catholic Relief Act. The event got out of hand and the ensuing week of disturbance came to be known as the Gordon Riots.*

Ecclesiastical, and, POLITIC

To the Respectable Association of Protestants & to every Worthy Supporter of both Church & State this Plate is Dedicated by their Humble Ser.t the Publisher.

state of the NATION.

40,000 English Protestants MASSACRED in Ireland 1641

PROTESTANT BURNT at Smithfield in the Reign of Queen MARY

Gunpowder Plot or an attempt to blow up the Parliament House

Protestants MASSACRED at Paris in the Vallies of PIEDMONT

WYE TRAPS

RIVER TWEED

EXPLANATION.

The State Husbandmen Plowing up the globe of the Constitution, whilst the Popish Emissaries, take the Advantage of the supineness of the Established Church, who is fast asleep in the Vineyard, where its grand Adversary the Pope, and all his host of DEVILS, are permitted to Sow the Seeds of their Pernicious Doctrine, Opposition attempts to stop their Progress, but the band of Unanimity is broke & they have fallen off. Truth, discovered, shewing a Scroll of melancholy proofs of popish cruelty, soliciting the Aid of her Friends to vanquish the Inveterate Enemy, who threatens the Ruin of their Religion, their Posterity, & their much injured Country.    Published June 2 1780 by H.B.

From 1778 onwards, the political pressure on North became acute. In a series of brilliant speeches Charles James Fox, third son of Henry Fox and a former junior member of the government, accused the Cabinet of 'a want of policy, of folly and madness'. North was condemned as 'a blundering pilot who had brought the nation into its present difficulties'. The government's disarray was clear to all in a debate on 2 February 1778 when Parliament had just returned. The House of Commons was crowded to hear Fox open the debate on the conduct of the war, and the government was so rattled that it ordered the galleries to be cleared. For two hours and forty minutes Fox landed such devastating blows upon the government that no minister got up to reply, but then North's obedient MPs gave him a clear majority of 106. A settlement with the American rebels was proposed but foundered on the matter of conceding independence.

The Whig opposition began to work as an organized body determined to bring the government down. They seized upon the issue of patronage, encouraged by the fact that in December 1779 a petition was presented to Parliament by a Yorkshire squire demanding a reduction of 'exorbitant emoluments' and the abolition of 'sinecure places and unmerited pensions'. The petition precipitated an avalanche of similar ones from across the country: the provinces had spoken and the spokesmen were the leaders of the middle class, local squires with a dislike of politicians. Nonetheless, Fox and the parliamentary Whigs seized the opportunity. As they were no longer in the running for sinecures and offices of profit, they demanded that these should be reduced or abolished, and that the power of the Crown should be limited (so-called economical reform). To put their case they recruited the golden pen of Edmund Burke, who in February 1780 delivered his famous Speech on Economical Reform. North was depicted in the prints as the controller of the flow of patronage but their real target was the personal power of the King.

Burke's plan was defeated but in April the same year John Dunning's famous motion – 'That the influence of the Crown has increased, is increasing, and ought to be diminished' – was carried by a majority of eighteen. The King was dangerously exposed. It is an exaggeration to claim that George wanted to create a personal despotism harking back to the Stuarts. In his utterances on America, he made the chief issue the right of Parliament to levy taxes. He believed, in his stubborn way, that the monarch had a role to protect, cherish and enhance the well-being of his countrymen, and to defend his nation's rights.

## A Great Man at his Private Devotion

10 June 1780

'PROTESTANT SCULPT'

*There was a spate of prints in 1779 and 1780 accusing George of being a Roman Catholic fellow-traveller. Protestants disliked the Quebec Act of 1774, which allowed Catholicism in Canada, and the very mild Catholic Relief Act of 1778. The King and Parliament were submerged in a flood of Protestant petitions – here they lie discarded 'for necessary uses', which means for the monarch's privy in the background. Above the door is a portrait of the Pope and beside it on the wall a torn print of Martin Luther. George is depicted as a monk praying before a Catholic altar, below a portrait of Lord Sandwich, nicknamed the 'Twitcher' after a character in the* Beggar's Opera, *and a picture of Lord North, entitled 'Boreas'. This print appeared just after nearly a week of destruction in London caused by the Gordon Riots: houses belonging to ministers and judges were burnt; the doors of jails were thrown open and over two thousand prisoners released; breweries were pillaged; Catholic schools, houses and chapels pulled down; and several hundred people were killed. Lord North and the City magistrates were so supine that George personally took charge as the 'one magistrate in the kingdom', summoning the Privy Council, which empowered the military to use force without the permission of a magistrate. Order was restored and anarchy checked. George was a devout Protestant but he was also the protector of his people. He was not prepared to see the centre of London destroyed by bands of Protestant fanatics.*

*A Great Man at his Private Devotion.*

Protestant sculp.

Published as the Act directs June 10th 1780 for proprietor, & Sold at No. 132 Fleet Street.

49

# 4 You Cannot Conquer America

THE PROBLEMS WITH the American colonies that George and his ministers had to face in the 1760s and 1770s were the problems of early imperialism. One of the most troubling aspects was the physical distance, some 3,000 miles, between America and Britain, so that messages or commands from London could take up to ten weeks to reach the colonies, but it was also a matter of distance of experience. No British politician – Chatham, Fox, North, Burke, Lord George Germain, Secretary of State for America, Lord Sandwich, First Lord of the Admiralty, nor the King himself – had ever set foot on American soil. George in particular derived his knowledge from those who returned to England and they were principally soldiers and governors. Unsurprisingly, the advice given directly to George was the advice of generals throughout history: if only we had more troops we will be able to control the country, bring them to heel, restore peace and preserve prosperity.

The source of the troubles was that governments of the 1760s and 1770s tried to find a way of getting the American colonies to contribute to the considerable cost of their protection and governance. As regiments of soldiers were shipped to America to protect the colonists against a resurgence of the French or attacks from the Indian tribes, it was considered not unreasonable for them to contribute towards that cost, but they saw little real benefit from this imposition of the British government. They also resented the requirement, by Acts of Parliament in 1765 and 1766, to quarter and billet the soldiers. A further source of aggravation was the Royal Proclamation of 1763, following a ferocious Indian uprising, which prohibited white settlement west of the Alleghenies. This rankled with the colonists, several of whom, including Benjamin Franklin and George Washington, had obtained grants of land across the mountains. In their view, the land and the profits they could derive from it were theirs.

At the heart of the crisis were ancient constitutional principles, namely that Britain as the mother country had the right to legislate for its offspring. Westminster was supreme and no politician, not even the Earl of Chatham, as the elder Pitt became in 1766, was prepared to abandon that principle. Only Burke had the imagination and foresight to realize that a much looser association was needed in order to retain the thirteen colonies. The British Commonwealth of Nations had to wait until 1926.

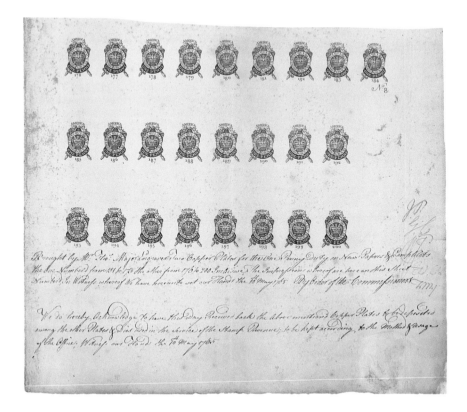

### The proof stamps for legal and commercial documents in America

1765

*These are proofs of the stamps that started Britain down the road to losing the American colonies. In 1765, George Grenville, with the enthusiastic support of George III, introduced a stamp tax on 'legal documents, newspapers, and other matters in America' similar to that in Britain. The stamps were to range in value from half a penny to £10 and were expected to raise £60,000 a year. In the event, not one stamp was ever sold in America.*

## The Repeal or The Funeral of Miss Ame-Stamp

18 March 1766

On the day that the Stamp Act was due to come into force, 1 November 1765, there was a riot in New York as it was seen as unconstitutional and unfair. Pitt condemned it eloquently, declaring 'I rejoice that America has resisted', but what really killed the tax were the petitions from the manufacturing towns – Birmingham, Manchester, Liverpool and Sheffield – which were alarmed by the American merchants' threat to boycott their goods. In February 1766, the new Prime Minister, the Marquis of Rockingham, decided to repeal the Act and George III was cheered in the streets.

In this print, published the day after the Act's repeal by the House of Lords, bales of stamps have been returned from America; a statue honouring Pitt is to be shipped there; one of the ships is named Rockingham, another Grafton, who was Secretary of State for the Northern Department; Grenville reluctantly carries the coffin of Miss Ame-Stamp to the family vault; Bute is the chief mourner; and the warehouses of the manufacturing towns are open for business again. The print was so popular that within four days of publication 2,000 copies had been sold and pirated copies from the fifth impression were bought in their thousands.

American colonists carried with them many of the instincts of the constitutional pioneers who had created the parliamentary system in England. They had a spirit of independence and of critical inquiry; a suspicion of an over-powerful monarch; and a devotion to free speech and the rule of law. The only political arrangement that may have suited them would have been some concept of a commonwealth, a free and self-governing association which was happy to recognize allegiance to one monarch, as all their traditions originated from the country over which that monarch reigned. But such a compromise, a possibility in 1763, had by 1775 become an impossibility through folly, ignorance and stubbornness. There were powerful forces at work, which would have crushed a greater man than George III.

The Grenville administration of 1763–65 proposed to share the cost of running the colonies with the colonies themselves. Grenville introduced a sugar tax on imported molasses, 'to raise revenue in America for defraying the expenses of defending,

## The Colonies Reduced

August 1768

POLITICAL REGISTER

*This prophetic print depicts Britannia being lopped of her limbs – her colonies; an olive branch has fallen from one hand and ships lie idle in the background. The* Political Register, *a sharp critic of the government's American policy, is here publishing an image attributed to Benjamin Franklin. He is reputed to have had it printed on cards that were handed to MPs before debates as a way of warning what would happen if Britain continued her coercive policies. The words 'Date Obolum Belisario', which loosely translate as 'spare a penny for Belisarius', refer to the legend of the sixth-century general whose eyes Justinian ordered to be put out, making him a homeless beggar. In 1767, the publication of Jean-François Marmontel's novel* Bélisaire *made the story a popular subject for progressive painters and their patrons who drew parallels between the actions of the Roman emperor and the repression of contemporary rulers.*

## The Bloody Massacre perpetrated in King Street, Boston

1770

PAUL REVERE

*Tension grew in Boston and on 5 March a hostile mob taunted a British sentry outside the Customs House. To protect him eight soldiers and an officer emerged from the guardhouse and within a few minutes five Americans were shot dead. This print is a blatant piece of propaganda. The redcoats did not line up and open fire and in the subsequent trial they were acquitted of murder and just two found guilty of manslaughter. Their defence lawyer, John Adams, a cousin of the leading anti-royalist Samuel Adams (the master of arranging rent-a-mobs), and later the second President of the United States, argued that they had been assaulted by a 'motley rabble of saucy boys, negroes and mulatoes, Irish teagues and outlandish jack tarrs'. This print was engraved and printed by Paul Revere, a silversmith, who became famous for his night ride on 18 April 1775 towards Concord bringing the news that the British army was preparing to attack. Another version of the print was sold in England with the title* The Friends of Arbitrary Power – or – the Bloody Massacre.

The BLOODY MASSACRE perpetrated in King——t Street BOSTON on March 1770 by a party of the 29th REGt

Unhappy Boston! see thy Sons deplore,
Thy hallow'd Walks besmear'd with guiltless Gore.
While faithless P——n and his savage Bands,
With murd'rous Rancour stretch their bloody Hands;
Like fierce Barbarians grinning o'er their Prey,
Approve the Carnage, and enjoy the Day.

If scalding drops from Rage from Anguish Wrung,
If speechless Sorrows lab'ring for a Tongue.
Or if a weeping World can ought appease
The plaintive Ghosts of Victims such as these;
The Patriot's copious Tears for each are shed,
A glorious Tribute which embalms the Dead.

But know, Fate summons to that awful Goal,
Where Justice strips the Murd'rer of his Soul:
Should venal C——ts the scandal of the Land,
Snatch the relentless Villain from her Hand.
Keen Execrations on this Plate inscrib'd,
Shall reach a Judge who never can be brib'd.

Engrav'd Printed & Sold by Paul Revere Boston

The unhappy Sufferers were Messrs Saml Gray, Saml Maverick, Jams Caldwell, Crispus Attucks & Patk Carr
Killed. Six wounded; two of them (Christr Monk & John Clark) Mortally

protecting and securing the same'. Then he introduced a stamp tax on a large number of documents ranging from newspapers and playing cards to legal documents and cargo lists. This led to riots in Boston where the houses of the collector of taxes and the Governor were ransacked. It also resulted in the first full-scale intercolonial congress to be convened on American initative, which met in New York in October 1765. The revolutionary machinery had started to turn. At Westminster, the elder Pitt and Burke both eloquently attacked the Stamp Act and in March 1766 it was repealed, to little effect as it was accompanied by the Declaratory Act, which asserted that Parliament had not renunciated the right to impose taxation upon the American colonies. The settlers seized upon a phrase that had first been coined in Ireland – one of Ireland's great gifts to America – 'No taxation without representation.'

## The able Doctor, or America Swallowing the Bitter Draught

1 May 1774

LONDON MAGAZINE

*As a punishment for the Boston Tea Party, in early 1774 North passed a series of Coercive Acts of which one was the Boston Port Bill, here sticking out of his pocket, to close the port of Boston until compensation for the destroyed tea was paid. General Gage closed the port on 1 June. America is held down by Mansfield, the Lord Chief Justice, while the lecherous Sandwich looks up her skirt. North force feeds her with tea, which she spews back in his face. Mansfield was not to live down what he said during the passage of the Bill, quoting Gustavus Adolphus: 'My lads, you see these men. If you do not kill them, they will kill us.' Britannia hides her face in shame while France and Spain, spotting an opportunity, look on with interest. Bute, whose influence is exaggerated, holds the sword of military law. Another disastrous step had been taken towards war.*

*The able Doctor, or America Swallowing the Bitter Draught.*

Die Zerstörung der Königlichen Bild Saule zu Neu Yorck | La Destruction de la Statue royale a Nouvelle Yorck

A Paris chez Basset Rue St Jacques

**La Destruction de la Statue royale a Nouvelle Yorck**

1776

One of the consequences of George committing himself so openly to the support of his ministers in suppressing the American rebellion was that he put himself right in the front line, a perfect target for verbal critics and satirists. Junius had recognized in 1771 the importance of retaining royal dignity through distancing the monarch from his political ministers: 'Public honour is security; the feather that adorns the royal bird supports its flight; strip him of his plumage, and you fix him to the earth.' By going into the forum George inevitably drew down upon himself the verbal lashing of the words of the Declaration of Independence on 4 July 1776. Five days later his gilded equestrian statue in New York was pulled down by the Sons of Liberty, an organization led by men of standing. It is interesting that in this French print, slaves as well as colonists are attacking the statue. An armaments factory at Litchfield, Connecticut turned the statue into 42,088 bullets for American rifles.

## Noddle-Island or How are we deceived

12 May 1776

M. DARLY

*Fighting broke out at Lexington and Concord in April 1775 and the American rebel militia laid siege to Boston. The first battle of the war was fought on the outskirts of Boston at Bunker Hill in June 1775. The British won but with an appalling toll of dead and wounded. Two weeks later George Washington arrived to take command of the rebels. They occupied Dorchester Heights, overlooking Boston, and trained captured cannons upon the city, which led to Howe's evacuation to Halifax, Nova Scotia on 4 March 1776. Four months later the Declaration of Independence was signed.*

*The print satirizes defeat: the Battle of Chelsea Creek and Noddle Island on the outskirts of Boston had been the rebels' first victory at the end of May 1775. The title contains a pun on Howe's name and a reference to a misleading account given in the official* London Gazette. *Walpole wrote, 'nobody was deceived'. The two armies fight it out in the elaborate coiffure. The British redcoats are flying flags decorated with an ass and a fool's cap on them. This incredible hairstyle, known as a pouf and sometimes a yard high, was popularized by Marie Antoinette and became the rage across Europe.*

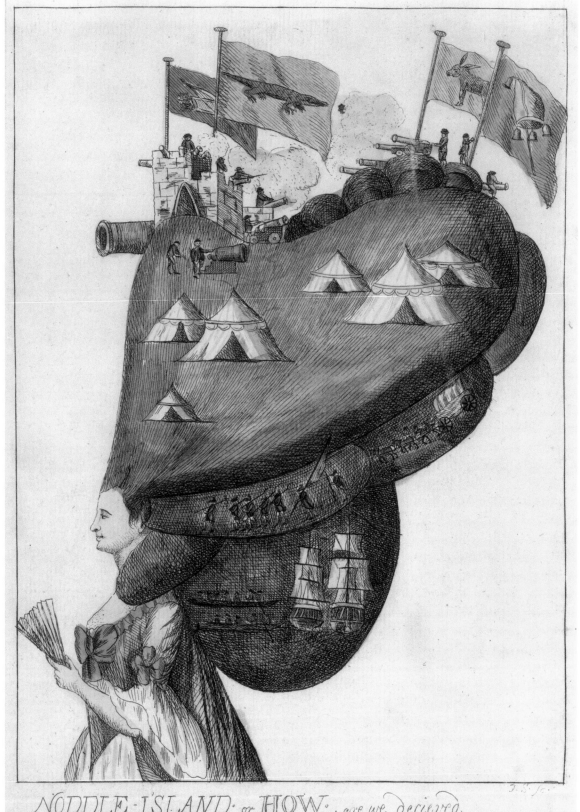

NODDLE·ISLAND· or HOW·. are we decieved.

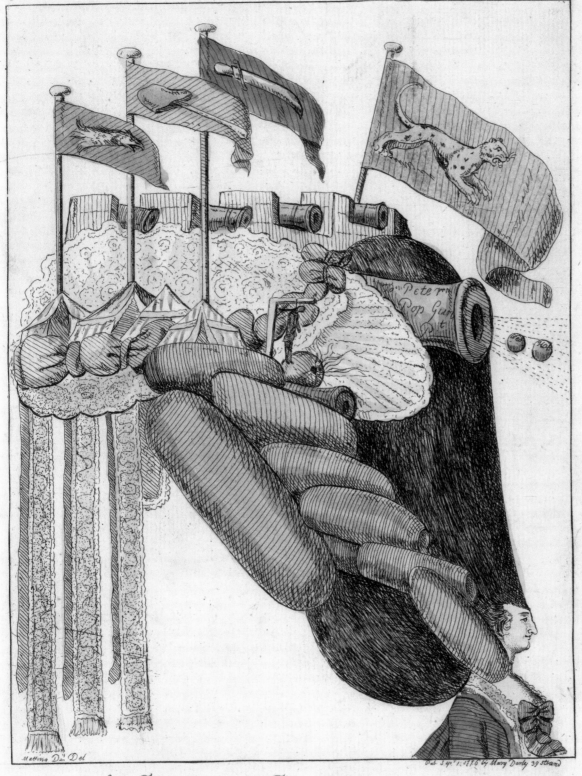

Mattino D.r Del

Pub. Sep. 1, 1776 by Mary Darly 39 strand

Miss CAROLINA·SULIVAN·

one of the obstinate daughters of America 1776

## Miss Carolina Sulivan one of the obstinate daughters of America, 1776

1 September 1776

MARY DARLY

*The governors of Virginia, North and South Carolina and Georgia hoped to raise bands of loyalists to support the British troops, but their hopes were dashed. The rebels won at Great Bridge in Virginia in December 1775 and Moores Creek Bridge in North Carolina in February 1776. With those states in rebel hands, a British fleet under Sir Peter Parker sailed to retake Charleston, South Carolina. The rebel spirits were roused by the arrival of General Charles Lee, who on 28 June resisted a combined sea and land assault on Sullivan's Island, which guarded the entrance to Charleston harbour. The British fleet was outshelled by the Charleston guns and three ships ran aground. The British General Henry Clinton had hoped to march his men through shallow water from neighbouring Long Island to Sullivan's Island, but found that the channel was too deep. It was a naval-military fiasco. It would be two years before the British renewed their campaign in the South. The cannon in Mrs Darly's print bears the name 'Peter Pop Gun', possibly a pun on the name of the British Admiral.*

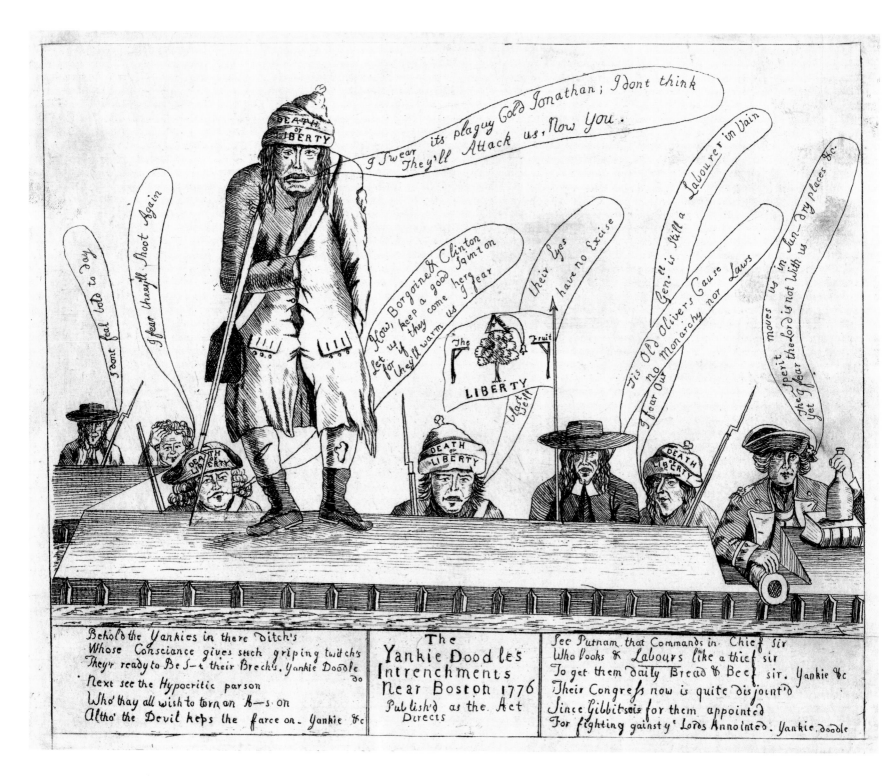

### The Yankie Doodles Intrenchments near Boston 1776

1776

*This is one of the few anti-American prints. The rag-tag, bob-tail army of Washington is depicted in all its sorry state, including one soldier who finds consolation in the bottle. The American general standing in rags on the palisade is Israel Putnam, who had fought at Bunker Hill. Washington's army was formed by groups of volunteers: there was no uniform, no willingness to obey orders, little training in firearms and a strong desire to return to their farms. Washington deplored the 'dirty mercenary spirit that pervades the whole' and at one point he said if he had known how bad they were he would never have accepted their command. During the long siege of Boston Washington fashioned these volunteers from the states into a fighting force: he imposed discipline, issued for the first time daily orders and fought strenuously to get better weapons and equipment.*

### Poor Old England endeavoring to reclaim his wicked American Children

1 April 1777

MATTHEW DARLY

*This print appeared not long after news reached London of Washington's winter victories at Trenton and Princeton. England is an angry, puzzled old man with a wooden leg, crutch and a cat-o'-nine-tails trying to control the young, confident, insolent and defiant Americans across the Atlantic Ocean. It would be over four years before George and his ministers realized that their task was impossible.*

Grenville's revenue-raising measures provoked resistance but the passage of the Townshend Acts in 1767 moved the colonies towards rebellion. Not only did they impose new import duties, but any violators were to be tried in the hated Admiralty courts. Customs officials requested the protection of British troops. Boston came to be run like a garrison for the British army and the presence of the redcoats was an incitement to riot. In 1770, when a street crowd jeered at some of them and threw stones, the troops fired back, killing five Bostonians and wounding others. This event was commemorated as a massacre for many years in Massachusetts every 5 March.

Boston, like many ports on the eastern seaboard, thrived through illegal smuggling – molasses from the West Indies and Dutch tea instead of East India Company tea. Attempts to collect more import duties were strongly resented but also cost more to impose than the revenue they could raise. This led to all duties being withdrawn but in May 1773 North insisted upon a tea tax. It was an ingenious way to reduce surplus East India Company tea piling up in London warehouses and to salvage the Company's finances. The duty would be lowered allowing tea to be sold for ten shillings instead of twenty shillings a pound thereby undercutting the smuggled tea. It seemed a bargain but it was too clever by half and had a sting in the tail: North insisted that the Tea Act should be imposed 'as a mark of the supremacy of Parliament'. George said: 'There must always be one tax to keep up the right. And as such I approve of the tea duty.'

By December, three British ships had entered Boston harbour with cargoes of East India Company tea; the Governor of Massachusetts ordered it be unloaded but the port workers refused. On 16 December a group of rebels disguised as Mohawks boarded the ships and threw the contents of 342 tea chests into the harbour. North's ministry responded in early 1774 with a series of punitive measures, including closing the port of Boston until the East India Company had been reimbursed. In a flash of prescience, Horace Walpole feared that 'our conduct has been that of hurt children, we have thrown a pebble at the mastiff and are surprised that it was not frightened. Now we must be worried by it or must kill the guardian of the house.'

The voices of dissent in Westminster – Fox asserting that 'countries should always be governed by the will of the governed', and Burke reflecting that 'magnanimity in politics is not seldom the truest mission' – were swept aside. They were out of step with the prevailing mood; 150 addresses from across the country were sent to George condemning the rebellious Americans. In September 1774, at the First Continental Congress in Philadelphia, the colonies refused to import British goods until their grievances had been answered. Samuel Johnson, in his pamphlet, *Taxation No Tyranny: An Answer to the Resolutions and Address of the American Congress*, argued that 'Our colonies...are entitled to all the rights of Englishmen. They are governed by English laws, entitled to English dignities, regulated by English counsels, and protected by English arms; and it seems to follow, by consequence not easily avoided, that they are subject to English government, and chargeable by English taxation.' This was a popular sentiment.

The King saw it as his duty to support his ministers and to uphold the rights of Parliament to tax. He also believed in 'the obedience which a colony owes to its mother country'. He was increasingly perceived to be taking a personal and decisive part in the policy of the government towards the American colonies. On 11 September 1774 he wrote: 'The dye is now cast, the colonies must either submit or triumph. I do not wish to come to severer measures, but we must not retreat...once vigorous measures appear to be the only means left of bringing the Americans to a due submission to the mother country the colonies

## Qualifying for a Campain

4 June 1777

*As this print was published before the battle of Saratoga it became a much more eloquent comment after the defeat in October. The British troops gossip in a relaxed way; fence with buttoned foils in hideous and cowardly postures; fire upon a castle of cards; and the only target they can hit is a tethered cat: not even the dog can be provoked to kill the rat that goads it. People in London were getting fed up with a war that was going nowhere, but one in which Britain had a better-trained and a better-equipped army.*

will submit.' His position had hardened by November to, 'blows must decide whether they are to be subject to this country or independent'. Others also realized that matters had come to a critical point. The historian and MP Edward Gibbon wrote that 'we have both the right and the power on our side and...we are now arrived at the decisive moment of preserving or of losing for ever both our trade and Empire.'

General Thomas Gage, who was married to an American, had told the King before he returned to America as commander-in-chief and Governor of Massachusetts that strong action was needed. Three other generals were despatched to help Gage: General Sir William Howe, personally courageous but a poor strategist, Lieutenant General 'Gentleman Johnny' Burgoyne, an adventurer, and General Sir Henry Clinton, lonely and aloof. Lord North commented, 'I don't know what the Americans will think of them, but I know that they make me tremble.' The generals throughout the war were a poor bunch: three spent more time philandering than fighting and one was actually found in bed with a Yankee 'doxey', but that did not prevent his later promotion. Meanwhile, thousands of colonists, many of them expert shots, had been assembling around Boston and amassing munitions. This led to the first skirmishes with Gage's redcoats at Lexington and Concord in April 1775 – the war had begun.

General Howe tried to raise the siege of Boston on 17 June 1775 by attacking the rebel position on Bunker Hill. This, the first battle of the war, was a Pyrrhic victory for the British. The Americans retreated from their position but they suffered 400 casualties compared to 1,100 of the British. Two days before,

QUALIFYING for a CAMPAIN.

London, Printed for R. Sayer & J. Bennett Map & Printsellers N? 53 Fleet Street, as the Act directs 4 June 1777.

the Second Continental Congress in Philadelphia had app-ointed George Washington to be commander-in-chief of the continental army and on 6 July the Congress adopted a 'Decla-ration of the Causes and Necessity of Taking up Arms'. The King, in his speech to open Parliament in October 1775 went on the attack. He would not permit 'an independent empire. I am unalterably determined at every hazard and at every risk of every consequence to compel the colonies to absolute submis-sion. It would be better totally to abandon them than to admit a single shadow of their doctrines.' He spoke with the confidence

of a leader of a nation who believed that he had a large, disci-plined, well-trained and well-equipped army. At the beginning of the war there were some 8,000 troops in America but it was a very inadequate force; many of the recruits were convicts or ex-smugglers. In 1776, the government had to look to Germany for five regiments from Hanover and others from George's family connections, including Hesse-Cassel, Mecklenburg-Strelitz and Brunswick-Wolfenbüttel; by the end of the war German merce-naries formed over one third of British strength in America, which then numbered 56,000 men.

## The Curious Zebra, alive From America! Walk in Gem'men and Ladies, walk in

3 September 1778

*The zebra is America and its stripes bear the names of the thirteen colonies. George Grenville is loading a saddle – the Stamp Act; North is holding the halter, declaring, 'I hold the Reins and will never quit them till the Beast is Subdued.' In the background are the three commissioners who had been sent to try to negotiate a peace settlement in the spring of 1778: Lord Carlisle, William Eden and George Johnstone, an MP and former governor of West Florida, who in the Commons had opposed the war. Eden says: 'Our Offers are Rejected, no terms but Independence.' This was the one point the British would not concede.*

*The figure in red on the right is a Frenchman who says, 'You are doing un grand Sottise, and Beggar I will avail myself of it.' The French had formed an alliance with the Americans that spring. The man in blue is George Washington, who says (alluding to his famous tactic of delaying full-scale battles with the British, following the example of the Roman general Fabius Maxiumus): 'My name is Fabius the Second, & the Rudder is my Hand. Pull Devil, Pull Baker, but She'll Stand upon her legs at last.' It is interesting that the printmaker in London did not turn him into a figure of ridicule or hatred, which was the way that Napoleon was treated later.*

Some nine months after the battle of Bunker Hill, British troops, after a long siege, had to evacuate Boston and on 18 March 1776 Washington marched in with colours flying. On 4 July 1776, the American leaders issued the Declaration of Independence in which the King, not Parliament, was deliberately singled out. As Samuel Adams wrote: 'I have heard that George III is his own minister. Why then should we cast odium upon his minions?' George was charged with twenty-eight crimes: 'He has plundered our seas, ravaged our coasts, burnt our towns, and destroyed the lives of our people'; he was 'a prince, whose character is thus marked by every act which may define a tyrant' and 'is unfit to be the ruler of a free people'. The rebels had to justify their rebellion and they needed a demon king – George helpfully provided the role. In this way, they indicated that they wished to cut every tie which connected them to the mother country.

There was some hope that the colonial uprising had been stopped in its tracks when General Howe attacked New York and took Long Island in August 1776. Washington's strategy, as he told Congress, was that 'we should on all occasions avoid a general action...unless compelled by a necessity'. He had to retreat over 180 miles through New Jersey to Pennsylvania and considered the game 'pretty much up', but realizing Howe's troops were spread too thinly he recrossed the Delaware to New Jersey on Christmas night 1776 and won dashing victories at Trenton and Princeton, which restored the morale of the rebel army and saved the revolution from collapse.

General Burgoyne returned to London on leave in the winter of 1776–77 and was so confident that he bet Charles James Fox a pony – the bet is recorded in Brooks's Club betting book – 'that he will be home victorious from America by Christmas 1777'. With Lord George Germain, the Secretary of State for America, he devised an elaborate plan to divide and conquer the rebels. He would lead a British army down the Hudson Valley from Canada while General Howe marched up from New York to meet him at Albany. This would cut off New England from the other colonies and the rebel states could then be picked off at leisure. A muddle over communications allowed Howe to capture Philadelphia, the rebel capital, which he believed was more strategically important. Unaware that he was on his own, Burgoyne started south in June 1777 and took Fort Ticonderoga – news that was jubilantly received in London. When George III heard of the victory he ran to the Queen shouting, 'I have beat them! Beat all the America[n]s'. The celebration was premature for within weeks Burgoyne's army was outnumbered three-to-one, supplies ran out, and on 17 October, surrounded by the

## The Political Raree-Show: The Generals in America doing nothing, or worse than nothing

June 1779

*WESTMINSTER MAGAZINE*

*In the summer of 1777, General John Burgoyne led an army south from Canada expecting to join at Albany, in upper New York State, a British army coming north up the Hudson River. After his initial success at Fort Ticonderoga in July, the rugged terrain and spirited attacks of the Americans, who destroyed a foraging party at Bennington, slowed him down. He crossed the Hudson River and it proved to be his Rubicon. Determined to keep going south, but with supplies diminishing, he encountered the Americans at the Battle of Bemis Heights in early October and sustained heavy casualties. His army, which then consisted of some 6,000 troops, including 2,400 German mercenaries, withdrew to Saratoga. The expected relief did not arrive. He was outnumbered by three to one and on 17 October he surrendered. Burgoyne told Gates, the American general: 'Your funds of men are inexhaustible. Like the Hydra's head*

*when cut off, seven more spring up in its stead.' As part of the surrender agreement, the British soldiers were to be allowed to return to England after pledging not to return to America, but Congress broke the deal, not trusting the British. All the troops were imprisoned until the end of the war. The news of Burgoyne's surrender reached London on 12 December 1777 and on hearing the news Chatham called the Americans 'Whigs in principle and heroes in conduct.' It was a turning point in the war since it encouraged France to enter on the Americans' side. In this image, one of twelve vignettes of recent events, Burgoyne is kneeling down to surrender the British flag. In the foreground another British general, with empty bottles at his feet, lounges at a card table. This is the pleasure-loving Sir William Howe, who had moved to take Philadelphia instead of heading north to meet Burgoyne.*

## The Allies – *Par nobile Fratrum!*

3 February 1780

In the Declaration of Independence the King was accused of having 'endeavoured to bring on the inhabitants of our frontiers, the merciless Indian savages, whose known rule of warfare is an undistinguished destruction of all ages, sexes, and conditions'. Benjamin Franklin, no less, forged letters implying that British officers had encouraged Native Americans to scalp the colonists for monetary rewards offered by George. With three Native Americans, depicted quite unfairly as cannibals, the King devours the remains of a baby. The whole world is turned upside down like the Bible at the base of the pole, and

in the flag 'Grace of God' and 'Defender of the Faith' are half-obscured. A bishop leads on a man delivering scalping knives, crucifixes and tomahawks as presents. Of all the satires this is the most personal attack upon George III. There is a deeper meaning, for Britain was often described as the Mother Country and the colonists as her rebellious children, so the charge against George is that he is cannibalizing his own young. This print also clearly blames the King as the prime mover of the whole British policy towards America.

American army, Burgoyne surrendered at Saratoga. Fox had won his bet. It was a turning point, as it precipitated France and subsequently Spain into war against their old enemy Britain.

From the beginning of the war the quality of American soldiers was totally underestimated. Lord Sandwich dismissed them as 'raw, undisciplined, cowardly men' and General Murray thought them effeminate. A young British officer in America told Germain that the rebels' cannons were 'excessively bad', their firearms 'very indifferent' and their legendary marksmen wasted their ammunition trying to pick-off redcoats. But after Saratoga one British officer wrote: 'The courage and obstinacy with which the Americans fought were the astonishment of every one, and we now become fully convinced, they are not that contemptible enemy we had hitherto imagined them.'

In London, Fox, Burke and Chatham led the campaign to end the war. In the Lords in November 1777, in what is considered his greatest speech, Chatham, although infirm, asserted: 'The conquest of English America is an impossibility…you cannot conquer America.' He went on to say that, 'If I were an American, as I am an Englishman, while a foreign troop was landed in my country, I never would lay down my arms – never – never – never.' In the Commons in February 1778 no minister rose to reply to a devastating speech by Fox criticising the management of the war, and North begged dozens of times to be allowed to resign on the grounds of ill health. The King would not hear of resignation and looked upon it as a personal betrayal.

The war dragged on and it was George's optimism that helped to keep it going. He wrote in December 1779: 'I do believe that America is nearer coming into temper to treat than perhaps at any other period.' Nonetheless, in October 1781 a French fleet of twenty warships reached Chesapeake Bay and on receiving this news Washington danced with delight. Caught between the French fleet and the Franco-American force, Cornwallis surrendered at Yorktown on 19 October. There were many in England who believed that the war should continue, including the King, but even those who supported the war recognized that England had been well and soundly defeated. Edward Gibbon's view changed: 'I shall never give my consent, to exhaust still further the finest country in the world in this prosecution of a war from whence no reasonable man entertains any hope of success. It is better to be humbled than ruined.'

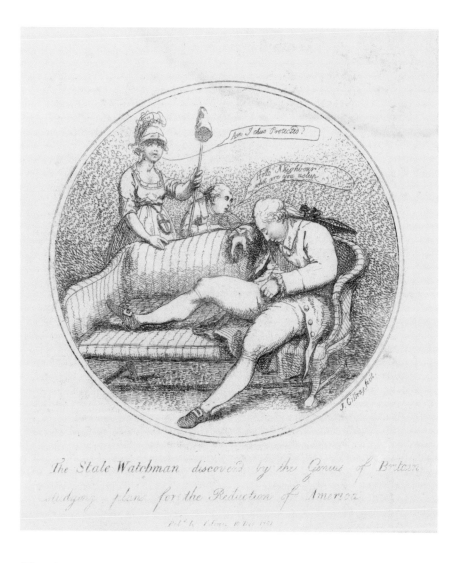

The Stale Watchman discovered by the Genius of Britain judging plans for the Reduction of America

**The State Watchman discovered by the Genius of Britain, studying plans for the Reduction of America**

10 December 1781

JAMES GILLRAY

*George yet again asleep at the post. Britannia rebukes him: 'Am I thus protected?' This print blames the King for Cornwallis's surrender at Yorktown on 19 October.*

**The Belligerant Plenipo's**

8 December 1782

*Peace negotiations had been going on between Britain and America since the spring and on 30 November preliminary articles were signed in Paris. America had won – here she stands smiling on the right, holding half of George's crown and saying, 'I have got all I wanted'. The French are fed up at gaining nothing for their support of the Americans, represented by the lost arm which lies at George's feet; the Dutch, in patched clothes reflecting their economic hardship, have lost a foot; Spain angrily demands Gibraltar in lieu of its lost leg; above them all Ireland demands her own constitutional freedom. George crossly declares, 'I give them independence.'*

## The General P—s, or Peace

16 January 1783

*The separate peace terms agreed between Britain, France and Spain were to be signed at Versailles on 20 January 1783, shortly after this print was produced. The five main participants of the war – Britain, Holland, America, Spain and France – are urinating into a pot while their flags, drums and swords lie discarded on the ground. Differences had to be buried, though France cannot resist a waspish retort: 'we have wrangled you out of America', and the Native American calls it 'a free and Independent P—'. The Englishman has to be content with: 'I call this an honourable P—.'*

## Blessed are the Peacemakers

24 February 1783

*In the ultimate humiliation Spain and France lead George by a halter through a gateway of spears from which the British lion, crown and unicorn are falling. He is followed by Lord Shelburne, the smug peace negotiator and Prime Minister since July 1782. They are scourged by America with a lash of thirteen tails who is leading a disconsolate Dutchman. On 21 February the Commons rejected Shelburne's peace terms, barely any members having a good word to say for him, and the next day George wrote, 'I am sorry it has been my lot to reign in the most profligate Age and when the most unatural [sic] coalition seems to have taken place, which can but add confusion and distraction among a too much divided Nation.' On the very day this print appeared Shelburne resigned.*

Blessed are the PEACE MAKERS

At the end of February 1782, the Commons voted to end all offensive warfare in America. 'The torrent', North wrote to the King in March, 'is too strong to be resisted...the Prince on the Throne cannot, with prudence, oppose the deliberate resolution of the House of Commons.' North said he must resign but George refused to accept that. On a censure motion in the Commons on 20 March, North said he had resigned, thus forcing the King's hand. George was furious: 'Remember, my lord, that it is you who desert me, not I you.' George was quite happy to blame everybody but himself. Just as the preliminary peace proposals were agreed in November 1782, he wrote to one of North's successors, Lord Shelburne: 'I cannot conclude without mentioning how sensibly I feel the dismemberment of America from this Empire, and that I should be miserable indeed if I did not feel that no blame on that account can be laid at my door.'

George, punctilious about diplomatic etiquette, had to receive in audience on 1 June 1785 the first American minister to the Court of St James, John Adams, who in 1797 was to succeed Washington as the second President of the United States. Adams, in a speech he had learnt by heart, spoke of reconciliation between 'people who, though separated by an ocean and under different governments, have the same language, a similar religion and kindred blood'. George was moved, but resilient to the last he replied, 'I wish you, Sir, to believe and that it be understood in America, that I have done nothing in the late contest but what I thought myself indispensably bound to do by the duty which I owe to my people. I will be very free with you, I was the last to consent to the separation; but the separation having been made and having become inevitable, I have always said, as I say now, that I would be the first to meet the friendship of the United States as an independent power.'

**The Savages let loose, or
The Cruel Fate of the
Loyalists**

March 1783

*The peace terms virtually abandoned the loyalists to penal legislation,
confiscation of their property and molestation at the hands of the
victorious Americans, represented here by Native Americans. Four
loyalists have been hanged from a branch with a sarcastic allusion to
Lord Shelburne and in the foregound two more are about to be scalped
and axed to death. One poor victim exclaims, 'O Cruel Fate! is this the
Return for Our Loyalty.' A contemporary squib made a similar point:*

> *'Tis an honor to serve the bravest of nations
> And to be left to be hanged in their capitulations.*

*But as with all conflicts: to the victors the spoils.*

## Plate 6 from 'America, A Prophecy'

1793

WILLIAM BLAKE

*Blake, no lover of regal power, in his poem* America, A Prophecy, *assigns much of the blame for the loss of the American colonies to George. The verse that precedes this illustration reads:*

> *...On his cliffs stood Albion's wrathful Prince,*
> *A dragon form, clashing his scales: at midnight he arose*
> *And flam'd red meteors round the land of Albion beneath;*
> *His voice, his locks, his awful shoulders, and his glowing eyes*
> *Appear to the Americans upon the cloudy night.*

*Various aspects of George's power are thought to be represented here: as the dragon, the 'Guardian Prince of Albion', sending down thunderbolts, and as the white-bearded figure, 'Albion's Angel', with tablets of law and the sceptre. The figures at the bottom cower before the double onslaught. The crouching figure who holds his hands over his head – a common gesture for a clouded mind – might allude to George's 'madness', which had become public knowledge in 1788–89. Later in the poem Blake describes the physical symptoms of George's insanity.*

# 5 Kill the Fox

IN MARCH 1782, a Whig administration headed by the Marquis of Rockingham succeeded Lord North. Its two leading figures were Charles James Fox and the Earl of Shelburne but there was little trust between them and the ministry soon ran into trouble. Shelburne took the King's side in the attempts to reform the royal household and Fox complained that the administration 'was to consist of two parts – one belonging to the King, one to the public'. They argued in particular over who should lead the peace negotiations with America. Fox as Foreign Secretary was responsible for the negotiations with the European powers but Shelburne as Secretary for Home and Colonial Affairs had the responsibility for dealing with the Americans. Fox said: 'Shelburne is ridiculously jealous of my encroaching on his department and wishes very much to encroach on mine.' The Cabinet voted to support Shelburne's position that American independence should be granted only as part of a general settlement. Fox threatened to resign but the very next day, 1 July, Rockingham succumbed to an influenza epidemic that was sweeping the country and died.

Fox, a charismatic figure, had attracted to himself a personal gathering of Whigs in the 1780 election and had earned the soubriquet 'The Man of the People'. An engaging and attractive personality, he was openly louche, a reckless gambler at the table and on the turf, attracted to duchesses and to the ladies of the town, fiercely loyal to his friends, wittily contemptuous of his enemies, but a brilliant orator who could always fill the House of Commons. The fastidious Horace Walpole, never at a loss for a waspish comment, observed that 'Fox lodged in St James's Street, and as soon as he rose, which was very late, had a levee of his followers, and of the gaming club at Brooks's – all his disciples. His bristly black person, and shagged breast quite open and rarely purified by any ablutions, was wrapped in a foul linen nightgown and his bushy hair dishevelled.' It is hardly surprising that he became one of the most frequently caricatured figures of his generation.

Fox was only too willing to wear a coat of buff and blue, the colours of Washington's army. He inspired tenacious personal loyalty but his followers had to forgive him a great deal, for he became as reckless in politics as he was at the gaming table, but when his debts could not be met they rallied round to pay them off.

**Guy Vaux**

30 March 1782

JAMES GILLRAY

*The Rockingham administration, after the torpid days of North, had a flavour of republicanism – it was at this time that Fox talked of George as 'Satan'. This print, with its allusion to Guy Fawkes, hints at something more sinister. Fox, carrying a dark lantern, leads the conspirators, including Shelburne holding a barrel of gunpowder and Richmond the faggots, as they break in upon the King. George is depicted as an ass wearing a dunce's cap and with his hands shackled. Fast asleep, he is not aware of the ministers threatening his authority.*

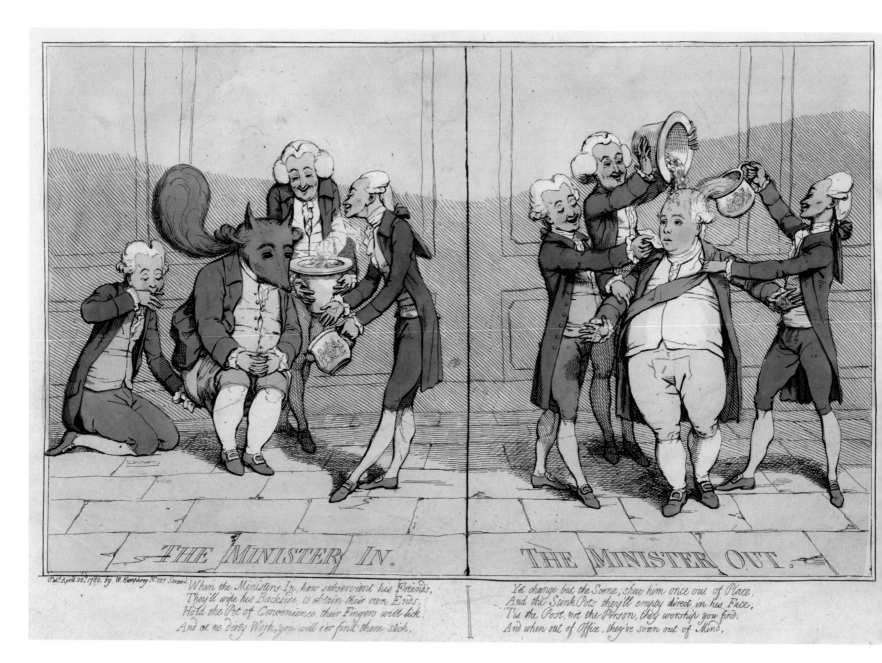

THE MINISTER IN.    THE MINISTER OUT.

Pub.<sup>d</sup> April 22. 1782. by W. Humphrey N.º 227 Strand.

When the Ministers In, how subservient his Friends,
They'll wipe his Backside, to obtain their own Ends,
Hold the Pot of Convenience, their Fingers will lick,
And at no dirty Work, you will e'er find them stick.

Yet change but the Scene, shew him once out of Place,
And the Stink Pots they'll empty direct in his Face,
'Tis the Post, not the Person, they worship you find,
And when out of Office, they're soon out of Mind.

**The Minister In.
The Minister
Out**

22 April 1782

JAMES GILLRAY

*A wry comment on the loss and acquisition of power. On 27 March the Marquis of Rockingham had replaced Lord North as First Lord of the Treasury. Fox was appointed Secretary of State for Foreign Affairs and it is he, not Rockingham, who is the star of the administration. Here, Fox is offered a chamber pot engraved with the royal arms, while a courtier wipes his bottom and yet another bears away a stinking pot. In contrast, North has the contents of two pots tipped over him. There were no qualms in the 18th century about bodily functions. The verse below Fox reads:*

> *When the Ministers In, how subservient his Friends,*
> *They'll wipe his Backside, to obtain their own Ends,*
> *Hold the Pot of Convenience, their Fingers will lick,*
> *And at no Dirty Work, you will e'er find them stick.*

He openly criticized George and remarked about his conduct of American policy: 'How intolerable that it should be in the power of one blockhead to do so much mischief.' The King was equally contemptuous, once declaring, 'That young man has so thoroughly cast off every principle of common honour and honesty that he must become as contemptible as he is odious.'

Upon the death of Rockingham, Fox wanted the King to appoint the Duke of Portland on the grounds that he had the support of the majority of the Cabinet and the ministry; Fox was essentially arguing against the royal prerogative of appointing ministers. Few people supported him and the King appointed Shelburne as First Lord of the Treasury, whereupon

## The Captive Prince – or – Liberty run Mad

23 April 1782

*Rockingham's brief ministry was intent on curbing the King's influence and reforming the Civil List. In this print the new Prime Minister walks off with the crown, George is being shackled at the wrists by Admiral Keppel, First Lord of the Admiralty and Fox's uncle the Duke of Richmond, Master-General of the Ordnance, and at his ankles by Fox and Lord John Cavendish, the Chancellor of the Exchequer. There are republican overtones in this print but it reflects the public's perception that George's power was being restrained by the new government.*

## The Political Mirror or an Exhibition of Ministers for April 1782

*Rockingham and members of his new ministry, including Fox, Richmond, Burke and the Lord Chancellor Thurlow, watch as the old regime – North holding a list of taxes, Sandwich a violin, Mansfield covering his eyes and Germain in the clutches of the devil – are falling into Hell. Britannia looks on from the left, declaring, 'They would have ruined me if they had staid in power.' Lord Bute also makes an appearance riding on a witch – this is extraordinary, as by then he was completely out of politics.*

Fox resigned. George observed, 'every honest man must wish to the utmost to keep him out of power.'

Shelburne's ministry, never strong, foundered on the terms of the peace settlement to the war. By February 1783 he had no friends in the Cabinet and no secure Parliamentary majority – Edward Gibbon stylishly noted the government's position *vis-à-vis* Fox and North: 'Ministers, 140; Reynard, 90; Boreas, 120, the rest unknown or uncertain.' Having appointed the younger Pitt as Chancellor of the Exchequer (at the age of only twenty-three), Shelburne asked him to find out if Fox would be willing

The POLITICAL MIRROR
or an EXHIBITION of MINISTERS for April 1782.

## Ecce!

1 October 1782

JAMES GILLRAY

*Shelburne had became First Lord of the Treasury in July, but alienated his Cabinet colleagues and lacked a convincing majority in the Commons – rumours soon abounded about his inevitable fall. George is overcome by melancholy as a hag of corruption sweeps away his crown. Lord North, only recently ousted, together with a few Tory ex-ministers including Sandwich on the extreme right, try to comfort the King, implying they are ready to take office again. The Latin motto above the print declares, 'The Rough with the Smooth'. This was the frontispiece for a poem,* The Beauties of Administration, *which contains the lines:*

> *When deep-laid plots of state, or war are*
>     *plann'd,*
> *Say are not N——th and S———ch both at*
>     *hand?*

to join the government. There was a celebrated and well-recorded exchange. When Pitt confirmed that Shelburne would remain as First Lord of the Treasury, Fox said, 'It is impossible for me to belong to any administration of which Lord Shelburne is the head.' Pitt replied, 'We need discuss the matter no further. I did not come here to betray Lord Shelburne.' From that moment the coolness started that was to become the greatest personal rivalry of the 18th century.

Rebuffed by Pitt, Fox realized that the only way he could return to office was to do a deal with Lord North, sacrificing his reputation, which had been built on radical reform and total opposition to North's Tory government. In 1779, Fox had called North 'a lump of deformity and disease, of folly and wickedness, of ignorance and temerity'. He defended his volte-face with these words: 'I am accused of having formed a junction with a

noble person whose principles I have been in the habit of opposing for the last seven years of my life. It is not in my nature to bear malice, or to live in ill-will....I disdain to keep alive in my bosom the enmities which I may bear to men when the cause of the enmities is no more.' He had attacked North over the American war but now that was over, so was his enmity. Few were convinced. However, by joining together they defeated Shelburne in February 1783. During the month of March George tried to persuade several politicians to take office in order to prevent the appointment of a Fox–North coalition. He even approached Pitt, who had been in the Commons for less than three years, but Pitt realized he would have had to rely on North and, unlike Fox, was not prepared to make compromises for power.

In April 1783, the King accepted the Duke of Portland as First Lord of the Treasury but it was Fox as Secretary of State for Foreign Affairs and North as Secretary of State for Home and Colonial Affairs who dominated the new ministry. This marriage of opposites became one of the most caricatured events of the 18th century. George did not conceal his opposition, not least because he detested Fox for his bad influence on the Prince of Wales and North for returning to government after years of begging to resign. He described the coalition as 'the most daring and unprincipled act that the annals of this kingdom ever produced'. He went further: 'It is impossible I would wish such a government would last....I hope many months will not elapse before the Grenvilles, the Pitts and other men of abilities and character will relieve me.' George even drafted a letter of abdication.

In spite of the coalition commanding a substantial majority in the Commons, George was determined to get rid of it. He had twenty-three years experience of dealing with political alliances that came and went and so he knew the strength of the cards he held. His ace was the firm refusal to give any peerages to the ever-demanding supporters of the coalition. He sensed that time would reveal its duplicity. Fox as Foreign Secretary had to commend to the House the terms of the American peace settlement which he had so eloquently opposed. The King's distrust of Fox was intensified when, during the summer, he sided with the Prince of Wales over the financial settlement of the Prince's income and payment of his debts. The Cabinet had proposed a payment of £100,000 (£7.1 million in today's money) a year once the heir to the throne became twenty-one in August and George thought half that amount was quite sufficient, being the sum he had received at the same age. He was not

on speaking terms with his son because of 'his total disobedience of every injunction I had given' and he expressed his 'utter indignation and astonishment' that his ministers, on what he saw as a family matter, did not accept his advice. George ended the exchange with an ominous threat that he would not 'forget or forgive what has passed', although he had been victorious – the Prince of Wales had to accept a settlement of £50,000 a year plus the Duchy of Cornwall income.

### The Sour Prospect before Us, or the Ins Throwing Up. State—Affairs. The Sweet Prospect behind Us, or the Outs in Office

April 1783

WILLIAM DENT

*In the first of this pair of prints, Shelburne's outgoing ministers are vomitting their signs of office, including Richmond, Master General of the Ordnance, in the centre and Thurlow, the Lord Chancellor, second from the right. In the second print, members of the coalition – Fox, North and Burke – and their friends – the Prince of Wales and Maria Fitzherbert – celebrate by defecating and farting upon the nation.*

The main measure of the autumn sitting of Parliament was the India Bill, drafted by Burke, to bring the government of India under closer public control. It was generally agreed that running the civil administration of a vast territory was too complex for the East India Company to manage. Its finances were in disarray and it depended upon a system of patronage, extortion and bribes. Ten years earlier, Horace Walpole had asked, 'What is England now? A sink of Indian wealth filled by Nabobs and emptied by Maccaronies.' (Nabobs was slang for Englishmen who had made fortunes in India, and a maccaroni was a fashionable spendthrift.) The Bill proposed a Commission for the Government of India, whose members would be nominated by Parliament, which effectively would mean the coalition. Fox's opponents depicted it as an attempt to get his hands on the vast patronage and revenues of the East India Company, which were greater than those of the Crown. In the 18th century patronage solved the problem of the younger son, so it was not surprising that one of the proposed commissioners was a son of Lord North, and it was said that the others were better known at Brooks's Club than in India – an ominous start. It was feared that Fox would abuse the powers of patronage in the way his father had done. Having tricked himself into office by abandoning his principles, Fox would be able to remain in power for as long as he wished.

The Bill, supported by Burke's great eloquence, was rushed through the Commons within a month. It had a majority of 109; Pitt's tirade against it did not persuade the country and non-party MPs. The India Bill, however, gave the King the chance to plan and implement a daring coup which was as dan-gerous and reckless as any of the political decisions that Fox had made. He could not defy a majority of the House of Commons, but he might influence the House of Lords and bring about the defeat of the government he disliked and whom he felt he would be in thrall to if the Bill were passed. His personal role in the overthrow of the Fox–North coalition would prove to be the most controversial individual act of his entire reign and provoked deep rancour among the Whigs.

Lord Thurlow, a former Lord Chancellor, who bore a grudge against Fox for not re-appointing him to that post, and Pitt's cousin, the second Earl Temple, encouraged George to make known to the House of Lords his views on the Bill. But George was wily and experienced enough to know that he had to have an alternative Prime Minister and in Pitt he saw his opportunity. So Lord Clarendon, an experienced former minister, and Count Alvensleben, the Hanoverian minister in London, were enrolled as go-betweens – loyal, discreet and obscure enough not to raise any suspicion of intrigue. Also involved in the plot were Henry Dundas, a friend of Pitt's in the Commons, Richard Atkinson, an India House director, and the Duke of Richmond. John Robinson, who had served in the Treasury under North and was the best party manager in the business, set about compiling lists of MPs who would support Pitt, and more crucially those who would have to be won over.

Rumours started to spread and Lord Frederick Cavendish told Georgiana, Duchess of Devonshire, that when the Duke of Portland, the nominal head of the government, got wind of these he challenged the King in his closet. George fixed him with a glassy stare and ignored the question. George then sent for

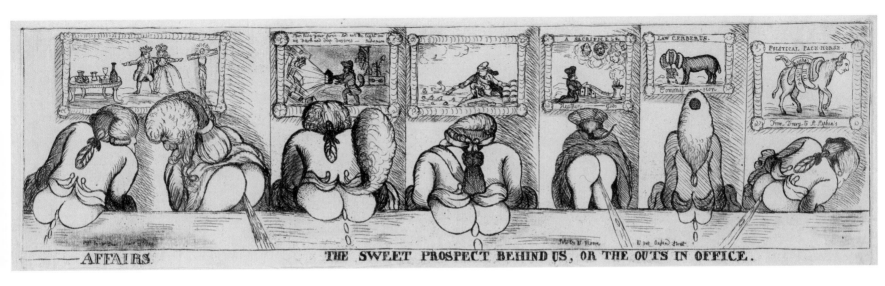

AFFAIRS.                THE SWEET PROSPECT BEHIND US, OR THE OUTS IN OFFICE.

## Junction of Parties

25 April 1783

JAMES GILLRAY

*During the American war Fox had called for North's impeachment and on one occasion said that if he ever had anything to do with any member of North's government he would 'rest satisfied to be called the most infamous of mankind'. Yet on 2 April they took office together under Portland's titular leadership. Even the devil is holding his nose as they both excrete into a pan bearing the royal arms. North is already the sleeping partner in his nightcap, but Fox has a more sinister intent in his 'gunpowder jowl'.*

## A Sun setting in a Fog: with the Old Hanover Hack descending

3 June 1783

JAMES GILLRAY

Fox was the dominant force of the coalition and within two months he was being compared to Cromwell. He is riding the horse of Hanover downhill into the Valley of Annihilation: the stirrups are broken, the reins have fallen to the ground to be replaced by a rope and moisture drops from the horse's eyes and mouth as Fox flogs it with a triple lash. The crown has been cast aside along with Magna Carta and George's head is simply a pillion passenger. Fox as Secretary of State for Foreign Affairs has had to carry through Shelburne's peace settlements of the American war and is accused of being pro-Spanish and pro-French – his boots are made of Spanish

leather and a French cock crows over the King's head. A document in the saddlebags is entitled 'French Commission' and on Fox's waistcoat he sports a fleur-de-lys. Gillray's title alludes to Shelburne's comment: 'The sun of Great Britain will set whenever she acknowledges the independence of America.' Prints like this one steeled George's determination to strike Fox down when the chance arose. George recognized that Fox was quick and had great eloquence but thought 'he wanted application and consequently the fundamental knowledge necessary for business, and above all was totally destitute of discretion and sound judgement'.

*A Sun setting in a Fog, with the Old Hanover Hack descending.*

## Carlo Khan's triumphal Entry into Leadenhall Street

5 December 1783

JAMES SAYERS

*This was published at the high point of Fox's campaign on the India Bill, which foundered later that month in the House of Lords after George's inteference. Fox, dressed as an oriental potentate enjoying the spoils of patronage, is drawn in triumph towards the East India Company's headquarters in the City. The elephant has the face of North and is led by Burke, the author of the Bill, who blows a trumpet. The motto on the flag, 'Man of the People', has been erased and replaced by the Greek inscription 'King of Kings'.*

*Writing to his long-term mistress and future wife, Elizabeth Armistead, Fox was realistic about the contentious nature of the bill: 'I am not at all ignorant of the political danger which I run by this bold measure' but he knew that he 'must bear the consequences, though I dislike unpopularity as much as any man.' Fox said this print did him more damage than any speech. The author, Sayers, was a lawyer turned propagandist for Pitt. This was his most famous caricature and it earned him the sinecure post of Marshal of the Court of Exchequer.*

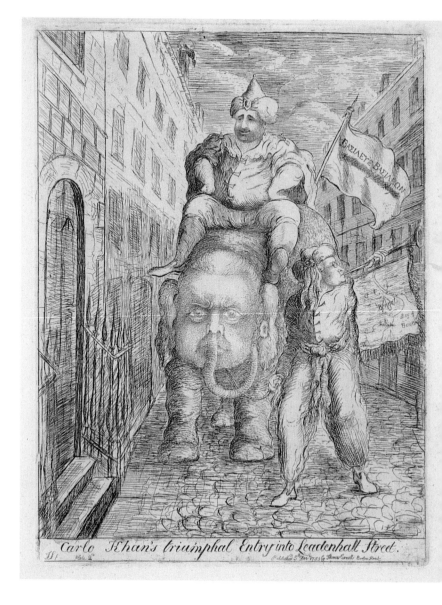

*Carlo Khan's triumphal Entry into Leadenhall Street.*

Lord Temple and gave him the following note to show to the members of the House of Lords: 'His Majesty allowed Earl Temple to say that whoever voted for the India Bill was not only not his friend, but would be considered by him as an enemy; and if these words were not strong enough, Earl Temple might use whatever words he might deem stronger and more to the purpose.'

Temple set to work. George, meantime, summoned the Archbishop of Canterbury for an audience and in due course a majority of the bishops voted against the Bill. At the second reading in the House of Lords on 17 December it was thrown out by 19 votes. In vain did Fox rage at 'such treachery on the part of the King' and declare that the Commons was to 'become the mere echo of secret influence'. Towards midnight on 18 December, Fox and North, meeting together, were informed by a special messenger that the King had no further use of their services and they were to surrender their seals of office to the courier, 'as audiences on such occasions must be unpleasant'. The next day Pitt accepted office as First Lord of the Treasury and Chancellor of the Exchequer – news greeted with derision; the new Prime Minister was only twenty-four. Fox predicted the government would not last much beyond Christmas, when he would divide against it, and Mrs Crewe, the celebrated Whig hostess, dubbed it the 'mince pie' administration.

## The rise of India Stock, & Sinking fund of Oppression

January 1784

*The King, standing before the scales labelled 'Right weighed against Oppression', cries: 'To preserve Justice, villainy must fall.' With a sword inscribed Prerogative he cuts down the Fox–North coalition and they fall into the Mire of Opposition. The house of the East India Company is supported by the King's left arm which is inscribed 'Government Security'. George's action to bring down a government that had a Commons majority of over one hundred was a quite exceptional exercise of royal power. It was not viewed by everyone in as favourable a light as depicted here. The* Morning Herald *of 19 January declared that 'The cloven foot of absolute monarchy begins to appear, as is evident when secret influence rises superior to the voice of the people in their representative body.'*

The rise of India Stock & Sinking fund of Oppression.

Fox should have insisted upon an immediate dissolution but he seems to have been surprised and simply could not believe that Pitt would survive without a sufficient number of votes in the Commons. Pitt's Cabinet was weak, composed of men who were less than second rate, and since they were all peers, he had to defend his policies in the Commons on his own. His particular friends, such as his cousin Grenville and Henry Dundas, held only junior places. It was as much a coalition as the previous ministry and as one wit said, it was united less by collective responsibility than 'a collective capacity for drink'. Nor did Pitt wish to ask for a dissolution at this stage, although a minority government was unusual. He wanted to build his support first.

John Robinson got busy with his target of turning around at least forty MPs. Three borough-owners, who controlled a number of seats, were made peers – as Walpole noted, the government was 'crying peerages about the streets in barrows'. Fox took the high ground, maintaining it was constitutionally unacceptable for the Crown to use its prerogative to sustain a government without a Commons majority. But this was the voice of the future. George argued that 'if the two only remaining privileges of the Crown are infringed, that of negativing Bills that have passed both Houses of Parliament, or that of naming the Ministers to be employed, I cannot but feel...that I can no longer be of utility to this country.'

Pitt simply denied that he was a 'tool of secret influence', but he certainly was. Public opinion, fanned by his supporters in the country and by subsidized newspapers and commentaries, began to turn in his favour. In February, when he received the freedom of the City of London, his carriage was drawn by crowds back to Westminster, and loyal addresses from towns flooded in. Wakefield's message came in a coach carrying a flag emblazoned in letters of gold, 'The King! The Constitution! The People! and Pitt for ever!' Furthermore, when Pitt's carriage was attacked by Fox's friends outside Brooks's Club, it did little to help the Whigs' cause.

The government's spin doctors had turned Fox into the enemy of the constitution, with Pitt as its saviour. Lord Palmerston noticed 'an epidemical kind of spirit that has gone about the country in favour of the King's prerogative and against the House of Commons.' Not only was Fox losing support in the country, but also in the Commons. In the first vote after Christmas, his majority was 39; in mid-February it was 12; and on 8 March it was 1. North's followers now supported Pitt. On 24 March, the day of the dissolution of Parliament, London papers predicted a Pitt victory in the forthcoming general election and Robinson expected a majority of seventy.

## Dissolution

6 February 1784

*In the early months of 1784 Fox and Pitt were locked in a parliamentary struggle as Fox manœuvred to defeat the minority government. The King, who is in a chariot with the slogan 'Mon Droit' on the wheel hub, is using his prerogative of dissolving Parliament, throwing Fox, North and Burke into the flames below. He is being driven by Pitt and his ministers. In fact, it would be another seven weeks before Pitt was ready to ask George to dissolve Parliament. Fox was just starting his long years in the opposition wilderness. He would come to regard the events of 1782–84 as the 'determining experience' of his career.*

Thunder of Dissolution

Mon Droit

iſolution

Pub.d as ye Act directs Feb.y 6 1784 by P. Walwyn
No 2 Pedlar's Acre West.r Bridge

A PEEP INTO FRIAR BACON'S STUDY.

Pub.d March 3 1784 by W Humphrey N 227. Strand.

## A Peep into Friar Bacon's Study

3 March 1784

THOMAS ROWLANDSON

*George III is depicted as Friar Bacon, the evil necromancer of Robert Greene's play,* Friar Bacon and Friar Bungay *(1594) in which Bacon created a great brass head with the power of speech that utters three phrases – 'Time was', 'Time is' and 'Time is past'. The three large circles portray three states of the constitution. The ideal one is on the right (Time was) when the King, Commons and Lords were equal; the one in the centre (Time is) shows the King bigger than the Lords, who in turn are larger than the Commons since the defeat of the India Bill; and the one on the left (Time is past) is a throwback to the absolute power of the monarchy, with the King dominant and the Lords and Commons just little balloons. George points with his sticks to the mini-Commons (centre) and to the absolute king, and says, 'What is this – To this'. He is getting too big for his royal boots. Little wonder that Fox shouts 'Beware' and Pitt's friends are led down the back stairs by a demon.*

The choice before the country was clear. Pitt was young, the son of a great Prime Minister and was seen as 'Honest Billy', having opposed the India Bill and proposed two motions for parliamentary reform; his ministry also had the advantage of holding office – no 18th-century government lost a general election. In contrast, Fox was thirty-five, his private life scandalous, and he had moved from being a radical reformer to tie himself to a man he had sworn to impeach. His judgement was reckless and he was perceived as having planned to set himself up in permanent power through the manipulation of Indian patronage. The differences were encapsulated by one observer of the two men's debating styles: 'Mr Pitt conceives his sentences before he utters them. Mr Fox throws himself into the middle of his, and leaves it to God Almighty to get him out again.'

The election that followed in April 1784 was one of the most bitterly fought of the century. Pitt told his friend William Wilberforce 'to tear the enemy to pieces'. It was not a battle of issues – it was simply a question of which personality would exercise power. The election lasted several weeks and there were constant allegations of bribery and fraud. The King told Pitt that as Fox had won with bad votes the Tories should do the same. Samuel Johnson remarked that the struggle was 'Whether the nation should be ruled by the sceptre of George Third or the tongue of Fox.'

Across the country the election was seen in the same light. The electors of York were asked 'George the Third or Charles Fox to reign?' The Treasury spent over £30,000 (£2.1 million) on the election; those who controlled seats were cajoled or threatened; and patronage – the great gift of an incumbent ministry – was liberally bestowed.

The battle for Fox's Westminster constituency became the focal point and it is said that a quarter of the total electoral expenditure was spent there. Fox was returned by a narrow margin but out of spite Pitt tried to prevent him taking his seat on a technicality. Nationally, the result was a Pitt landslide. The celebrities of the day, the Duchesses of Devonshire and Portland, who had openly canvassed for Fox by offering kisses to the butchers and shoemakers of Westminster, were devastated. The 160 supporters of the Fox–North coalition who had lost their seats were dubbed 'Fox's martyrs'. When the new Parliament met in May, Pitt's majority in the debate on the Address was 282 to 114. The 'mince pie' administration was starting seventeen years of uninterrupted power.

THE ROYAL HERCULES Destroying THE DRAGON PYTHON

### The Royal Hercules Destroying The Dragon Python

24 April 1784

*The prints in the early months of 1784 were overwhelmingly against Fox and for the King and Pitt. Here the King is struggling with Fox, North and Burke. It is ironic that George, in manipulating the defeat of the Fox–North coalition, was seen as the saviour of the constitution. From now on he began to regain some of the popularity with which he had begun his reign.*

# 6 The Bottomless Pitt

IN GEORGE III'S REIGN the role of Prime Minister emerged out of that of chief minister to the Crown. Originally, the king had been a member of the Cabinet, but as George I did not speak English and George II was frequently out of the country that practice had fallen into disuse and was not renewed by George III.

In 1721, Robert Walpole started his twenty-one-year tenure as First Lord of the Treasury and chief minister of George I and George II. He is generally regarded as Britain's first Prime Minister although he disowned the title when he was attacked for having too much power. Under George III, both Grenville and Lord North rejected the title since it was the king as head of the government who had to approve the appointment of the ministers, each of whom had direct access to the Crown.

It was William Pitt the Younger, First Lord of the Treasury from 1783 to 1801 and again in the years 1804 to 1806, who effectively shaped the role of Prime Minister, helped by the decline of the King's influence on day-to-day matters due to his age, his periodic illness and his willingness to leave things to Pitt. The last chief minister appointed by George III, just before his illness in 1810, was Spencer Perceval; by this time, the term had become generally accepted and Perceval was quite happy to use the title of Prime Minister.

Pitt had a meteoric rise to power, aided by the disaster of the American war. He started by lying and continued with bribery. He told the House of Commons:

I came up no back stair. When I was sent for by my Sovereign to know whether I would accept office I necessarily went to the Royal Closet. I know of no secret influence, and I hope that my own integrity would be my guardian against that danger....Little did I think to be even charged in this House with being the tool and shelter of secret influence.

This was a lie from start to finish but as none of the plotters was going to correct the record he got away with it. From the beginning his pose was as a man of complete integrity and the world took him at his own valuation. His coolness under the scornful fire of Fox was pivotal to the survival of his government for the key months of December 1783 to March 1784. However, it needed a good deal more. The support of the King meant that he held the key to the door of patronage and to secure a majority in the Commons not a farthing was spared. His cousin Thomas Pitt received a peerage; James Lowther, a boroughmonger with nine votes, was promised an earldom; a peerage for the second son of the Duke of Northumberland secured seven more seats; Lord Weymouth switched sides when his brother was ennobled; a royal pension for the wife of a near-bankrupt MP secured his support; and the father of Edward Eliot, Pitt's

### The First Levee of the New P—r—t [Parliament]

29 May 1784

*To secure a parliamentary majority Pitt had to offer posts, pensions, sinecures and peerages. His fixer was John Robinson, known as the Ratcatcher (note the rat on his forehead), because he bribed MPs to rat. Pitt draws his followers on reins down the road to preferment to kiss the bare posterior of the King. Peerages were given to boroughmongers; men with Irish and Scottish titles were elevated to full mark. Some had been 'representative' peers, but most had not been peers. George needed Pitt to overthrow Fox, and Pitt needed George as the fountain of patronage – the floodgates had to be opened. Pitt never shrank from bribery but he left it to others to do the dirty work. Robinson was rewarded by seeing the father of his son-in-law raised to the earldom of Abergavenny.*

ILLUSTRATION BY SHADE.

### Illustration by Shade

May 1788

WILLIAM DENT

*The impeachment of Warren Hastings over his ruthless methods in India is underway. This print aims to show the truth behind the views taken by the leading figures. Hastings, at the centre, turbaned and in Oriental dress, holds a sword inscribed 'Justice' but his 'true shadow' depicts him as a devil with an axe inscribed 'Perversion'. The King and the Lord Chancellor, Thurlow, both opposed the impeachment. George's shadow transposes his crown into a 'bulse', a packet for carrying diamonds, as two years earlier he had been given a valuable diamond by Hastings. Thurlow's great bag of the seal of office is transformed into bags of gold, implying that he had been bribed by Hastings. At the far end, the Home Secretary, Lord Sydney, becomes a headless 'Tom Fool'. Pitt's shadow is more interesting. He is not accused of corruption but the key he is holding is to the Back Stairs, implying his secret influence with the King. Dent depicts Pitt's shadow once again as a girl, hinting at his sexual passivity.*

*An epigram in an opposition paper ran:*

*'For Pitt so young,' cries Ned, 'just twenty-five,
Why don't the women make a fuss?'
'A fuss for him!' quoth Nell. 'Why man alive,
He never stands up for us.'*

Election-Troops, bringing in their accounts, to the Pay-Table..

**Election-Troops, bringing in their accounts, to the Pay-Table**

14 August 1788

JAMES GILLRAY

*The Westminster by-election in July–August 1788 was fiercely contested. The Whigs, who were alleged to have spent £50,000 (£2.1 million), won the day. The expenses of the Pittite candidate were met by a whip-round of ministers; the Treasury made up the balance. Here Edward Topham, owner of the pro-government newspaper, the* World, *presents a bill to Pitt who tells him 'to go to the back door in Great George Street under the Rose'. George Rose had taken over from Robinson at the Treasury as dispenser of election funds. There is an amusing collection of electoral malpractices: 'For Puffs & Squibs and for abusing opposition', 'For changing Sides' and 'For Voting 3 Times'. This contest cost so much that in the general election of 1790 the two parties did a deal over this seat. It is possible that Gillray had not received his own fee and this was his revenge.*

friend, got a peerage for a further six seats in Cornwall. The King joined in as well, persuading the Duke of Newcastle to have three of his MPs switch sides and the other three to abstain.

Britain after the American war was demoralized, defensive and divided. Pitt asserted his authority in a series of budgets that restored the economy, reduced the national debt and strengthened the navy. But he also had some major setbacks. He had to abandon his proposed reforms of Parliament when a majority of MPs declined to vote for measures that would rob them of their 'rotten boroughs'. Neither his eloquence nor his handling of the Commons could persuade them to support the proposals of his friend William Wilberforce to abolish slavery.

Pitt strengthened his position in two ways. First, by promoting talented young men, including two future Prime Ministers: George Canning and Robert Jenkinson, subsequently Lord Liverpool. After eight years, Pitt was strong enough to force George III to dismiss Thurlow, the Lord Chancellor, a giant of the past who believed he had created Pitt, but had showed him neither loyalty nor respect. Secondly, Pitt split the Whigs. By 1794 many of the Whig leaders were appalled by the excesses in France and their earlier revolutionary sympathy ebbed. Pitt acted quickly and persuaded the leader of the Whig moderates, Portland, to join his government, and several MPs also crossed the floor. The radical Whigs led by Fox were reduced to a mere rump of fifty MPs and they were condemned to be in opposition for twenty-seven of the next twenty-eight years.

Pitt devoted all his energies and his time to the government of the country. He had few outside interests apart from shooting partridge and drinking large quantities of port with his friends, particularly Henry Dundas. He made no attempt to feather his own pocket and the King had to thrust upon him the sinecure post of Lord Warden of the Cinque Ports. While Pitt put the nation's finances in order, his own were chaotic and his instinctive generosity led to a life of debt.

## A Proclamation in Lilliput

22 May 1792

RICHARD NEWTON

*A royal proclamation of 21 May 1792 sought to suppress 'all loose and licentious Prints, Books and Publications, dispensing Poison to the Minds of the Young and Unwary; and to punish the Publishers and Vendors thereof'. Pitt, wearing a clown's hat, reads out a parody: 'Who ever after this our will and pleasure, dares to look, walk, stand, write, sit, speak, act, think, run, eat, drink, sleep, evacuate piss, or committing any other misdemeanour... shall forthwith be bash'd, boil'd, stew'd, roasted, fricasseed etc., according to the utmost limits and bounds of our supreme wisdom.' George had at last found a minister, 'Billy, read read on my boy', who was totally attuned to his own views. George used his royal prerogative to issue proclamations in the way today's prime ministers and presidents use the 'bully pulpit' to appeal to the public when they cannot secure the passage of a Bill.*

A Proclamation in Lilliput

## The Fall of the Wolsey of the Woolsack

24 May 1792

JAMES GILLRAY

By 1792, Pitt, assisted by his cousin Lord Grenville, was strong enough to sack Thurlow, the Lord Chancellor, but the King was reluctant to abandon an old friend. Thurlow was arrogant, vain and conceited, after all he was the king-maker who led the conspiracy that deposed Fox and installed Pitt in 1783. In April 1792, he publicly opposed both Pitt's Bill to fund new public loans that would reduce the national debt and the proposals to abolish the slave trade. On 16 May Pitt told the King to choose between himself and the Chancellor. George had no choice, Thurlow had to go.

## Sin, Death, and the Devil

9 June 1792

JAMES GILLRAY

This struggle of the Titans is based upon Milton's Paradise Lost: Pitt is Death wearing the King's crown and directing his spear against Thurlow, who as Satan is defending himself with a shield decorated with the Great Seal. The Queen is the Snaky Sorceress, Sin, defending Pitt, who apparently had her favour, and her right hand is suggestively placed over his private parts, even possibly encouraging them. She is a hideous hag with snakes for hair, pendulous breasts and legs like the tails of serpents. This is the most offensive caricature of Charlotte and it was deeply resented by the royal family. The three-headed Cerberus is (from the top), Charles Lennox, Duke of Richmond, Master-General of the Ordnance, Lord Grenville, Foreign Secretary, and Henry Dundas, Home Secretary. Gillray's image of Sin, Death and the Devil parodies paintings by Hogarth and Fuseli.

black it stood as night,
Fierce as ten Furies, terrible as hell,
And shook a dreadfull dart: what seem'd his head
The likeness of a Kingly crown had on.;
Hell trembled at his hideous name.

She seem'd a Woman to the waist
But ended foul in many a scaly fold,
Voluminous and vast; a serpent arm'd
With mortal sting: about her middle round

A cry of Hell-hounds never ceasing bark'd
With wide Cerberian mouths full loud, & rung
A hideous peal: yet, when they list, would creep,
If ought disturb'd their noise, into her womb,
And kennel there.

Incens'd with indignation Satan stood
Unterrif'd: — but under brows
Of dauntless courage, & considrate pride
Waiting revenge:

NB: The above performance containing Portraits of the Devil, & his relations, drawn from the Life, is recommended to Meſsrs Boydell, Fuzelli &c. the rest of the Proprietors of the Three Hundred & Sixty Five Editions of Milton, now publishing, as necessary to be adopted in their classick Embellishments.

SIN, DEATH, and the DEVIL. Vide Milton.

" So Frown'd the mighty combatants, that hell
" Grew darker at their frown:— And now great deeds
" Had been atchievd, whereof all hell had rung

" Had not the Snaky-Sorceress that sat
" Fast by hell-gate, and kept the fatal Key,
" Ris'n, and with hideous outcry rush'd between.

Pub: June 9th 1792.
by H. Humphrey
Nº 18. Old Bond Street.

A Batch of Peers.

## A Batch of Peers

6 January 1793

RICHARD NEWTON

*At this time Pitt's ascendancy was complete and here George III, assisted by Charlotte, ennobles all the names submitted to him. By 1792, Pitt had created forty-three English peerages and ultimately would create eighty-nine, thereby increasing the size of the House of Lords by forty per cent. Britain was on the brink of war with France and in debates from December 1792 Fox could muster only fifty votes; he was isolated and denigrated as a Jacobin and a republican sympathizer. Pitt was at pains to recruit the moderate Whigs led by the Duke of Portland and several peerages were given to them. By 1794, forty Whigs had defected to Pitt: Portland became Home Secretary; William Windham, in the Commons, became War Secretary; and two Whig earls – Spencer and Fitzwilliam – also joined the Cabinet. The Pitt–Portland coalition formed the basis of the Tory Party as it developed over the next hundred years.*

## Britannia between Scylla & Charybdis

8 April 1793

JAMES GILLRAY

*Pitt is guiding Britannia in a small boat named* The Constitution *between the whirlpool of arbitrary power in the shape of an inverted crown and the rocks of French democracy, followed by the dogs of Scylla: Sheridan, Fox and Joseph Priestley. His destination is the castle flying the flag of the 'Haven of Public Happiness'. This anticipates Canning lauding Pitt as 'the pilot that weathered the storm'. Pitt's calmness saw the country through the crisis of the execution of Louis XVI in January and the French declaration of war upon England on 1 February. It was, however, the Whigs who were in trouble. Fox's speech in February opposing the war with France made him very unpopular and henceforth he was depicted somewhat unfairly as a republican. There was the added difficulty of his debts, which had grown so large that the only solution was for his friends to rally round and to pay them. Gillray's allusion to the Scylla and Charybdis of Homer's* Odyssey *would have been understood by all educated Englishmen of the period.*

SHARKS; *Dogs of Scylla.*

**BRITANNIA** *between* **SCYLLA** & **CHARYBDIS**.

OR — *The Vessel of the Constitution steered clear of the Rock of Democracy, and the Whirlpool of Arbitary-Power.*

Pub.d April 8.th 1793. by H. Humphrey, N.18 Old Bond Street

J.s G.y des.t et fec.t pro bono publico.

**George III and the Officers of State Receiving the Turkish Ambassador and Suit**

*An engraving after a painting by the American-born painter Mather Brown. Gillray had other ideas.*

**Presentation of the Mahometan Credentials – or – The final resource of French Atheists**

26 December 1793

JAMES GILLRAY

*Gillray again draws attention to Pitt's sexual passivity – showing him as a little mannequin shrinking before the visible manhood of the Turkish ambassador. One of the Prince of Wales's cronies wrote a song,* The Plenipotentiary:

> *When to England he came with his p—k in a flame*
> *He showed it his hostess at landing,*
> *Who spread its renown through all parts of town*
> *As a pintle past all understanding…*
> *When he came to the court, oh! what giggle and sport!*
> *Such squinting and squeezing to view him!…*

Presentation of the Mahometan Credentials — or — The final resource of French Atheists.

## A Puzzle of Portraits, Or the Hour Glass exhausted

10 February 1794

ISAAC CRUIKSHANK

*The sand in the hourglass between the profiles of Pitt and George is running out, as the war against the French is going badly. In Flanders, the British, commanded at George's insistence by the inadequate Duke of York, have been thrown back in disarray. In the south of France, a British force occupying Toulon has been ousted by an ardent young officer named Napoleon. In Paris, the Terror is at its height. Pitt's government is unpopular. A sinister threat can be found in this print; the hourglass's struts are human bones. Might the heads of Pitt and the King fall into the basket of a guillotine?*

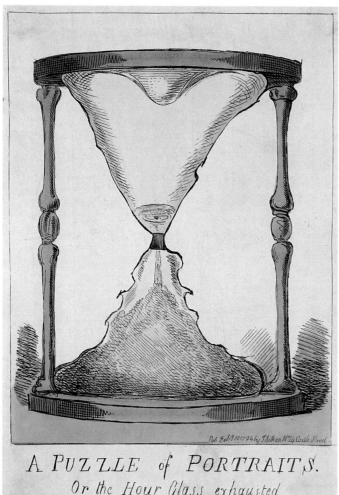

A PUZZLE of PORTRAITS.
Or the Hour Glass exhausted.

RITE CHICKENS,
*or the*
*nny's Farm-yard in* 1794

## Favorite Chickens or the State of Johnny's Farm-yard in 1794

1 October 1794

HEWITT

*George III, as a down-at-heel John Bull whose house is burning, is showering the Prussian eagles with gold – they had received their first subsidy from Britain in May. The Russian bear looks on greedily; the white horse of Hanover has its snout in the trough; and the British lion lies shackled while a Gallic cock pecks at his eyes. This reflects the collapse of the alliance against France in 1794. Charles IV of Spain returned to Madrid; Francis II of Austria went back to Vienna; William II of Prussia, in spite of the bribery, was more interested in grabbing what he could from the partition of Poland; and British troops in Flanders had been further humiliated.*

**Dressing the Minister, Alias Roasting the Guinea Pig**

23 May 1795

This is an interesting reminder of how unpopular Pitt became for introducing a hair-powder tax to help pay off the Prince of Wales's debts. After its introduction on 6 May everyone who wore a powdered wig had to pay a guinea (about £70) for a licence. The lists of licence holders – 'guinea pigs' – were to be posted on the door of parish churches. George, seen as the head of a wig-stand, rather apprehensively observes his Prime Minister being roasted. Pitt's tax harmed the barbers' trade and it was soon abandoned.

## Farmer George's Wonderful Monkey

2 July 1795

WILLIAM O'KEEFE

*In the summer of 1795, Pitt's government was in deep trouble. The King had asked Parliament to settle the Prince of Wales's debts; there were riots over the high price of bread following the poor harvest of 1794; the war was going badly – in June the Quiberon expedition to take back that part of Brittany had failed; Pitt's powder tax on wigs was unpopular and his budget had increased duties on wine, spirits, tea, coffee, cocoa, and stamps on receipts, affidavits and wills. In these months Pitt was caricatured as a sleepwalker, a pig, a locust, a caterpillar and a goblin. The Irish caricaturist William O'Keefe, whose vigorous works are often overlooked, depicts Pitt as the King's monkey, 'an Offspring of the Devil'. O'Keefe belittles Pitt as an instrument of the royal will.*

FARMER GEORGE'S WONDERFUL MONKEY

The Naturalists of this Country is at a Loss how to give an Account of this Extroardionary Animal, therefore we may Suppose it to be an Offspring of the Devils, & that he = Shit it Flying.

July 2d

Pub.d by J. Aitken Castle Street Leicester-Fields 1795

## A Contest Between Oppression & Reason, Or the Best way of Settleing Debates

7 November 1795

WILLIAM O'KEEFE

*Military failures, new and higher taxes and a poor harvest hit Pitt. His house was attacked and at times he needed a military escort. He was not deterred from taking a hard line against radical protests and introduced the Seditious Meetings Bill, whereby meetings of over fifty persons had to be authorized by a magistrate. He was strongly attacked by Fox and Sheridan. Here, supported by claret, he exchanges blows with Sheridan, supported by brandy, but there is no doubt that he has the full backing of the pugilistic King. The Bill received Royal Assent on 18 December.*

Nov.ʳ 7: 1795 Pub. by J. Aitken Castle Street Leicester Square                    W.O.K. Inv.

## A CONTEST

### BETWEEN OPPRESSION & REASON, OR THE BEST WAY of SETTLEING DEBATES

## The Royal Extinguisher or Gulliver Putting out the Patriots of Lilliput!!!

1 December 1795

ISAAC CRUIKSHANK

Pitt, dressed as a night-watchman with a rattle in his belt, his blue coat echoing the Windsor uniform of the King, directs the light of his lantern onto the leading Whigs, including Fox, Sheridan and Lord Stanhope, whose activities he is about to extinguish. The belt around them refers to Copenhagen Fields in Islington, the site of a mass meeting of radicals on 13 November. They had demanded annual parliaments and universal male suffrage. Earlier, on 29 October, the King's coach was attacked on its way to the opening of Parliament and the government feared that general unrest was about to break out. At the time this print appeared the Treasonable Practices and Seditious Meetings Bills, the so-called Gagging Acts, were nearing completion of their passage through Parliament.

The DISSOLUTION, — or — The Alchymist producing an Ætherial Representation.

## The Dissolution – or – The Alchemist producing an Aetherial Representation

21 May 1796

JAMES GILLRAY

*By the summer of 1796 Parliament had run six of its seven years and Pitt decided to dissolve it on 19 May before the situation overseas became any worse. Gillray portrays Pitt like an alchemist of old transforming Parliament, aided by the tools of his trade. With the help of the bellows of royal influence – Pitt is wearing the King's Windsor uniform of a blue coat with red facings – and the Treasury 'cole' (gold), the Prime Minister becomes the 'Perpetual Dictator', trampling on Magna Carta while Britannia's shield lies broken in a pestle and mortar. The government won the election, as it always did in the 18th century. Pitt ended up with 424 government supporters, 95 opposition and 39 independents. No other Prime Minister in the 18th century had such a commanding position.*

## Treason!!!

19 March 1798

RICHARD NEWTON

*George rigorously supported Pitt's measures against the radicals: the suspension of Habeas Corpus; the prosecution of the London Corresponding Society, which was agitating for parliamentary reform; the insistence of the death penalty for the mutineers of 1797 and 1798. He thought it right for Fox to be thrown out of the Privy Council for the toast at a Whig dinner to 'Our Sovereign, the People'. The year 1798 was singularly dangerous as there was a major, though unsuccessful rebellion in Ireland, and the fear that France would launch an invasion. It was brave, therefore, for the young Richard Newton to show John Bull, the representative of the poor British worker, mooning and farting at an image of the King – any criticsm was treason. Newton was lucky not to be prosecuted.*

# 7 The Madness

GEORGE WAS NO STRANGER to troublesome ailments. In 1762, he was ill with pains in his limbs and stomach, but being young and strong he shrugged them off. On 12 January 1765 he was taken ill with what appeared to be a feverish cold. He complained of 'stitches' in the chest and received the usual treatment of the period – blood-letting, repeated several times. It had no effect. In March, the King's pulse rate was 120, his face livid and his manner peculiar. George Grenville, the Prime Minister, decided that a Regency Bill was necessary and some ministers close to the King believed he was dying of an incurable 'consumption'. In his message to Parliament requesting arrangements for a regency he spoke of 'my late Indisposition, tho' not attended with danger'. There was widespread alarm that if George were

to die the Regent could well be his mother, which would have heralded the return of Bute. This provoked such fear that George reluctantly accepted Grenville's advice that his mother should be omitted from the list of possible Regents. When this leaked out there was a general reaction in favour of Augusta and the government had to reinstate her name. After the sickness in 1765 George enjoyed good health for over twenty years.

In June 1788, George had a severe bilious attack and his doctors recommended that he take the waters at Cheltenham. When he returned to London in August he was brought down by severe stomach pains and cramps in his legs; a red rash appeared on his arms. The doctors did not know what to do. In October, Sir George Baker, his principal doctor, was summoned to the

A SCENE at CHELTENHAM.

King's bedside after a particularly bad attack. George was subjected to strong laxatives, followed by laudanum, which counteracted their effect. On 22 October he was so angry with Baker about his medicines that the physician wrote to Pitt saying the King was close to delirium. His attendance at a levee on 24 October was alarming: his speech was slurred and thinking muddled. He went to Windsor where, according to Fanny Burney, he assured everybody of his health and was 'all benevolence and goodness'. However, she went on to record that there was 'a rapidity, a hoarseness of voice, a volubility, an earnestness – a vehemence, rather'; he told her that he did not sleep, 'not one minute, all night'. His behaviour became more and more erratic and he talked uncontrollably.

On 5 November, when the Prince of Wales came to dinner, his father suddenly rose from the table and in a great rage seized the Prince by the collar, pulled him out of his chair and threw him against a wall. The following day his eyes were like blackcurrant jelly, the veins in his face were swollen, the sound of his voice was dreadful, he foamed at the mouth. He was clearly deranged. He gave orders to people who were long dead or did not exist; he lavished honours on all and sundry; he told his daughters that he would take them to Hanover and marry them off to German princes; and one day he talked incessantly for nineteen hours. More doctors were called and everything was tried: leeches applied to his forehead; strong purges and emetics followed by sedatives. On 6 November he was given James's powder, a compound of antimony, to reduce fever. But after awaking from a deep sleep he had 'all the gestures and ravings of the most confirmed maniac'.

REVOLUTIONISTS.

## A Scene at Cheltenham

28 July 1788

*The King and his family went to Cheltenham to take the waters because he had been showing troubling symptoms. With his usual enthusiasm, he woke early and reached the well by six in the morning, where his impulsive and eccentric behaviour was noticed – and inspired this scene. Charlotte and two of his daughters try to drag him away from the pump. This print comes just three months before the full onset of his 'madness'.*

## Revolutionists

30 October 1788

WILLIAM DENT

*Just six days after George's eccentric behaviour at a levee had given cause for concern, Dent suggests that the Whigs see this as an opportunity for an assault on the Crown itself. They are led by Fox wielding an axe bearing the name 'Cromwell'; Sheridan has 'Wit' sticking out of his pocket; the Hon. George Hanger, a crony of the Prince of Wales, carries his master's standard; and Burke bears a cross. They mount an assault on the constitution itself, surmounted by the King representing the 'public good'.*

DEAD. POSITIVELY DEAD.

## Dead. Positively Dead

16 November 1788

HENRY KINGSBURY

*This is the first print to expose the crisis created by George III's illness. The Prince of Wales tramples on a paper, 'Prayer for Restorat[io]n his ——— Health', while Sheridan, the dramatist and leading Whig, carries dispatches for Charles James Fox, who was absent in Italy. Maria Fitzherbert's friends crown her queen. The Tory Thurlow plays a double game – here aligning himself with the Prince's cause by turning his coat – 'This side will do as well as the other.' At this date, rumours abounded of George's impending death.*

## Filial Piety

25 November 1788

THOMAS ROWLANDSON

*This is the only print that depicts George in his 'madness'. During a dinner on 5 November the King had assaulted the Prince of Wales and by the end of the month his condition had deteriorated to such an extent that the Prince had high hopes of becoming Regent. Here the drunken Prince bursts into the King's bedchamber followed by his cronies, the Hon. George Hanger, carrying a bottle, and Sheridan, who was intriguing to secure a regency and the Whigs return to power.*

In his poem *America, A Prophecy*, William Blake, who held George responsible for the loss of the colonies, graphically described his illness:

The red fires rag'd! the plagues recoil'd! then roll'd they
    back with fury
On Albion's Angels: then the Pestilence began in streaks
    of red
Across the limbs of Albion's Guardian…
Albion's Guardian writhed in torment on the eastern sky,

Pale, quiv'ring toward the brain his glimmering eyes,
    teeth chattering,
Howling & shuddering, his legs quivering, convuls'd
    each muscle & sinew

At the end of November the King was moved, against his wishes, from Windsor to Kew, to be nearer London and to be in a place where he could take exercise out of the public eye. On 5 December, another doctor, Dr Francis Willis, a seventy-year-old clergyman and physician who specialized in treating lunatics,

### A Touch on the Times

29 December 1788

THOMAS ROWLANDSON

This is the other side of the story. The Prince, looking forward to becoming King, is assisted up the stairs to the coronation chair by a cloven-hoofed Britannia. Sheridan, in rags, picks George's pocket; Fox holds up the scales of justice formed by two diceboxes; and Pitt tries to snuff out rebellion. The bag above the word VIRTUE on the back of the chair is a leather condom. Pitt insisted on limiting a regent's powers and in February 1789 his Regency Bill passed from the Commons to the Lords. It was assumed that the Prince was about to become Regent but George had started to recover and the Prince's hopes were dashed.

was summoned from Lincolnshire. Willis's principal treatment was to put his charges into a straitjacket whenever they did anything wrong. George was also confined to a specially made chair – his 'coronation chair' as he called it; restraint was necessary since George was physically violent and on at least one occasion he tried to throw himself out of a window.

During his periods of lucidity George was rather in awe of Willis but he came to dislike him profoundly. Nonetheless, Willis's treatment was more effective than any of the other doctors. Willis allowed the King certain privileges such as shaving himself, and Flora, his spaniel, was brought to him from Windsor.

For Pitt, the deterioration in the King's condition led to a political crisis. If George were to die the Prince of Wales as king would dismiss him and appoint a Whig administration, headed by Fox or Portland. London newspapers went so far as to publish lists of Whig ministers, and some prints depicted Pitt as a tyrant seizing the power of the Crown. Thomas Rowlandson was persuaded to change sides and drew prints supporting the Prince. If, on the other hand, George continued to live in his demented state, the Prince would have to become Regent. In that case, Pitt was determined that Parliament should limit his powers. Pitt was briefed on the King's condition by Willis and the Prince was kept informed by Dr Richard Warren, a Whig. They issued daily bulletins and the whole nation was aware of the King's deteriorating condition.

Pitt played for time by appointing a parliamentary commission – a well-known delaying manœuvre – to examine the doctors' reports. He then adjourned Parliament for a fortnight and appointed another committee to examine precedents. It became clear that provision for a regency would have to be made and on 10 December the Commons began to debate the whole issue. Fox incautiously overplayed his hand by claiming that the Prince had an inherent right to become regent and parliamentary approval was not needed. Pitt pounced on this, depicting Fox as the enemy of the constitution and on 12 February 1789 he secured the passage through the Commons of the Regency Bill, with restrictions on the Regent's powers, by a majority of sixty four. It now passed to the House of Lords.

While Parliament debated, the King's condition fluctuated. On 12 January one of George's doctors told the Lord Chancellor that he did not think the King would ever recover. Willis, on the other hand, was more optimistic, telling the committee appointed to examine the King's physicians that he had not 'the least doubt of his recovery'. Pitt's playing for time had worked. The King was indeed slowly recovering: on 10 February the bul-

## St Stephen's Mad-House; or the Inauguration of King William the Fourth

27 January 1789

*The madness of the King has afflicted the House of Commons. Pitt is mad, crowned as William IV with wisps of straw, and proclaims that 'Nelly Rogers shall be Queen'. He is congratulated by the Corporations of Puddledock, Hockley-in-the-Hole, etc. Dundas reminds him that the Weird Sisters promised him everything. One madman holds a coronet of straw and another sells 'Coronets a Shilling, Stars and Garters Sixpence'. Fox and Burke flee. Many prints showed Pitt grabbing the crown but this one goes further: he is not only corrupt by selling peerages but just as mad and dangerous as George III.*

letins spoke of the King as having passed 'the day before in a state of composure'; on 11 February, he was 'better this morning than he was yesterday'. On 15 February, even Dr Warren agreed that 'he might be said to be well'. The following week Lord Thurlow told their lordships that 'it would be indecent to proceed further with the Bill, when it might become wholly unnecessary'. It was effectively dead.

George was physically altered by the illness. He had lost weight; his face was said to be 'sharp as a knife'; he had grown a beard; he appeared 'extremely weak in his manner of walking';

London Published by William Holland, Printseller, No. 50 Oxford Street, April 29, 1789.

Just Pub.d Old Maids of Quality at a Cats Funeral; Irish Ambassadors Extraordinary; Irish Ambassadors returning to Dublin; An Irish Bull bait in England &c, &c.

### The Grand Procession to St Paul's

29 April 1789

THOMAS ROWLANDSON

*The Archbishop of Canterbury tried to dissuade George from going to St Paul's on St George's Day (23 April) to celebrate his recovery as it would take too much out of him. George replied, 'My Lord, I have twice read over the evidence of the physicians on my case, and if I can stand that I can stand anything.' The crowds sang 'God Save the King'; Pitt was cheered; the Prince of Wales was jeered; and Fox was hissed. George was visibly moved when several hundred children of the charity schools in the City 'set up their little voices and sang part of the Hundredth Psalm'.*

and his conduct had terrified his wife and daughters. The experience had turned Charlotte's hair from brown to white. It was a watershed in both his personal and political life. The illness helped to transform George into a popular and well-loved figure whom the people did not want to lose. In a burst of royalist affection, the nation rejoiced at his recovery with great parties and fireworks. The country was glad that this stubborn, old, awkward man who had been their sovereign for nearly thirty years had recovered. A baker woman in Sidmouth told Fanny Burney how a portrait of the King was mounted in a coach with eight horses and followed by all the 'grand gentlemen of the town in their own carriages....And they had the finest band of music in all England, singing God Save the King, & every soul joined in the Chorus – & all because not so much for a being

In Holland's Caricature Exhibition Rooms, may be seen the largest Collection of Political and other humorous Prints–admittance 1 Shilling

spect before us; St Stephens Mad House; Going in State to the House of Peers; Male Butchers; The Corporation of Roch–er returning from Carl–n House; The Vice Q–ns delivery in Dublin, &c.

THE GRAND PROCESSION to St PAUL'S

he was a King, but because they said as he was such a worthy Gentleman, & that the like of un was never known in this nation before.'

It was not until the 20th century that George's illness was diagnosed as porphyria, an hereditary disease that had been passed down through the royal line from Mary, Queen of Scots. There was no effective cure as it was unknown in the 18th century. Porphyria's symptoms include mental illness, abdominal pain, vomiting, constipation, weakness of the limbs, nausea and a characteristic dark-coloured urine. George's attacks were unusually serious and may have been brought on by traces of arsenic in the James's wig powder that he was given. Or it could have been his diet: in 2005, a team at Harvard Medical School identified the protein PGC-1a, which can become overactive in the liver, building up toxins in the blood and triggering porphyria. This protein is produced when the body is starved of glucose because of fasting and poor diet: so George's modest eating habits – his boiled eggs, bread and butter, muffins, and tea without sugar – may well have contributed to his illness. What George needed was carbohydrates and glucose – the very things that he refused to take. Nonetheless, there was the genetic element to his illness.

George's recovery was slow. He obeyed Dr Willis's advice to 'take a few dips in the sea'. He went to Weymouth, despite the long journey, where his brother the Duke of Gloucester had a house. On the way people from the villages and towns turned out to cheer their king. On 7 July, George's bathing-machine, with windows inscribed in gold with 'God Save the King,' was rolled down the beach into the waves, and as he descended into the sea a band struck up the national anthem.

In the early months of 1801 George had a relapse and two doctor-sons of Francis Willis were summoned. There were the usual symptoms and on 2 March the King's pulse rose to such a rapid rate that death was anticipated; the Prince of Wales and the Prime Minister were both called. His recovery was slow and by the end of March he was still unable to appear in public, though his ministers declared he was well, and had him perform some functions in private. In April, he ordered the Willises out, and tried to escape to Kew, but they caught up with him and applied the straitjacket.

The Willises kept George a virtual prisoner, refusing to let the Queen and her daughters see him. They hoped to secure a permanent position of power over the King and their disgraceful behaviour ended only when George told Lord Eldon, the Lord Chancellor, that he refused to sign any government papers unless he could see his family. During the summer he went to Weymouth and slowly got better. The Queen told their son Prince Augustus that the King was 'much better and stronger for

the sea bathing'. By November, George was able to tell Dr Hurd, Bishop of Worcester, that 'I feel I am gradually gaining ground.' But the illness had taken its toll. The diplomat Lord Malmesbury noted, 'he appeared rather more of an old man….He stooped rather more, and was apparently less firm on his legs.'

A third serious attack occurred in 1804. George's mind was sufficiently agitated for the Cabinet, who had assumed responsibility for the health of the King, to summon the Willises yet again. On the night of 14 February his fever was very high and he talked incessantly for five hours. The Speaker of the Commons thought he had succumbed to 'a complete mental derangement'. But the Dukes of Kent and Cumberland insisted that seeing the Willises would only aggravate George's condition. It was Henry Addington, then briefly Prime Minister, who sent instead for a physician from St Luke's Hospital for Lunaticks, Dr Samuel Simmons, who immediately put the King in a straitjacket. George was deemed well enough by May, however, to accept the resignation of Addington and he reappointed Pitt. But the King's behaviour continued to be erratic and Pitt observed 'His Majesty's hurry of spirits' and 'excessive love of talking'.

Royal Dipping.
Of purest Air, and healing Waves we tell,
Where, welcome Maid, Hygeia loves to dwell!
In Holland's Exhibition Rooms may be seen the largest Collection in Europe of Humorous Prints. Admittance, One Shilling.
London, Pub'd by Will.m Holland, N.o 50 Oxford Street
July 15, 1789

### Royal Dipping

15 July 1789

JOHN NIXON

*In July, George took his family on an extended holiday to the Dorset resort of Weymouth, having been told that seabathing would be good for his health. Here Charlotte and one of the princesses watch the royal descent into the waves. George's shaved head, common for lunatics at that time, reminds the public of his recent bout of insanity. A band, looking distinctly queasy, strikes up. On 13 July Fanny Burney noted in her diary, 'Think but of the surprise of His Majesty, the first time of his bathing, he had no sooner popped his royal head under the water, than a band of music, concealed in a neighbouring machine struck up "God save Great George our King".'*

## Wierd-Sisters: Ministers of Darkness: Minions of the Moon

23 December 1791

JAMES GILLRAY

*Although this print is dated 1791, according to the memoirs of Sir Nathanial Wraxall, a contemporary MP, it appeared in February 1789 during the regency crisis. Either way, it clearly records George's temporary insanity in 1788–89. The three ministers are Dundas, the Home Secretary, Pitt, the Prime Minister, and Thurlow, the Lord Chancellor, who gaze intensely and apprehensively at the moon, which displays the Queen's smiling profile on its bright side while the sleeping King is in darkness. The anxious ministers nervously stroke their chins, for if the King succumbs to permanent madness the Prince of Wales would become Regent and appoint a government of his Whig friends. Gillray in the superscription recognizes his debt to Henry Fuseli's famous 1783 painting of the witches from* Macbeth, the Weird Sisters, *which was popularized by an engraving issued in 1785.*

George also developed a great aversion to the Queen, which was noted by the Prince of Wales's secretary, John McMahon. He was also acting inappropriately towards women. The Queen and the princesses now travelled in a separate carriage 'having found it impossible to control the King to any propriety of conduct in their own coach'. Charlotte's feelings now ranged between fear and disgust. She locked the bedroom door against him and kept either her servants or her daughters by her until George went to bed. Since the Queen would no longer pleasure him, he threatened to take a mistress, possibly the Duchess of Rutland.

George went to Weymouth and began a slow recovery, but it was reported that he made lewd advances in public to ladies there and in the fish market he talked so incoherently that the fishwives 'scarcely believed they had their own senses'. He made indecent suggestions to one of the Queen's ladies and in the stables at Windsor his behaviour had been noted as 'indecent and obscene'. Rumours circulated, but there were so many along these lines that there must have been some truth in them. The recovery was patchy.

George was now an old man and finding it more and more difficult to recover from these attacks. He lost the sight in his left eye and wore a green eye shield. To recognize people he had to peer at them with his strange protuberant eyes close to their faces. He talked even more rapidly and moved bewilderingly from one subject to another. On returning to Windsor, the King and Queen lived in different parts of the castle. Princess Sophia, who was closer to her father than any of his other daughters, came to loathe her mother. She wrote to a friend, when the King was visiting Blackheath one time, that 'The old lady [the Queen] is in high glee, I suppose at the dear man's absence – How unnatural, how odious!' And again, 'The Queen's manner to the Angel is, in a word, shameful. Indeed I believe she has lost her head and her heart for I am sure it is as hard as a stone.'

George's eyesight continued to fail and from 1805 he was unable to read letters, so all government business had to be read out to him. He did what he could to appear on important state occasions. On 23 April 1805, he and all his sons attended a splendid procession of the Knights of the Garter at St George's Chapel, Windsor, a response to Napoleon's assumption of the title of Emperor the previous year. On that occasion the King wore a huge flowing wig, the sort that had been fashionable sixty or seventy years earlier.

# 8 George Split Farthing

THROUGHOUT THE REIGN, Gillray and other caricaturists dwelt on George's parsimony. However, it was the King's thriftiness when he ascended the throne that set him on a troubled course. He renounced most of his hereditary revenue to Parliament in return for a fixed annual income of £800,000 (£57 million in today's money), raised to £900,000 in 1777. This was a less generous arrangement than the one George II had enjoyed. The whole question of royal income has long been shrouded in obscurity, but at this time the Civil List was intended to pay for certain aspects of civil government (as opposed to military expenditure) as well as the royal household. Debts inevitably built up, incurred in part by George's growing family, and periodically the King reluctantly had to go back to Parliament for financial relief.

The Civil List Act of 1782 imposed some controls on royal expenditure, but in 1786 the King was asking Parliament to clear debts of £210,000. On 7 April *The Times* published a list of debts paid on previous occasions:

| | |
|---|---|
| 1769 | £ 513,511 |
| 1777 | £ 618,340 |
| 1781 | £ 433,893 |
| Total | £1,565,744 |

Including the latest request, this made a total debt in the first twenty-five years of the reign of £1,775,744 (nearly £127 million today).

*The Times* added: 'His Majesty's income has been stated by certain calculators to be nearly as follows':

| | |
|---|---|
| Civil List | £ 900,000 |
| From Hanover | £ 100,000 |
| From Ireland | £ 90,000 |
| From Wales | £ 10,000 |
| From Lancaster | £ 20,000 |
| Interest on debts due to HM | £ 150,000 |
| Total | £1,270,000 |

George was bitterly resentful of the blatant extravagance and unseemly behaviour of his son, the Prince of Wales. The King had to ask Lord North to find £5,000 (£350,000) to buy back the Prince's love letters from Mary Robinson, one of his first conquests. When the Prince came of age in 1783 the King

## The Mother and the Child

1 February 1773

*LONDON MAGAZINE*

*George is a suckling babe in the arms of Britannia. As the Privy Purse is empty he begs for 'more Supplies'. The* London Magazine *ran a 'Fragment of a Speech' that carried this comment: 'Our mother BRITAIN, has been drained of her nourishment till she is ready to expire…yet her SON, her best-beloved, her eldest-born, still hangs upon her breasts, still suckles, and (barbarous!) still shrieks out for "More Supplies! More Supplies!" Unnatural Boy!'*

## A new way to pay the National-Debt

21 April 1786

JAMES GILLRAY

In 1786, Pitt persuaded the Commons to grant £210,000 (£15 million) to discharge the latest debts on the Civil List. Outside the gates of the Treasury, George takes the bags of golden guineas offered by Pitt, who retains some in his own pocket. The King's clothes are bulging with golden guineas, as is the skirt of Charlotte, who takes snuff while looking admiringly at her husband. The obsequious musicians are placemen and courtiers who are also pocketing coins. In the foreground an armless and legless sailor is ignored. The Prince of Wales, in tattered clothes, is trying to negotiate a loan from his friend the Duc d'Orléans, one of the richest men in Europe (guillotined during the Terror in 1793). Fox failed to get relief for the Prince's much larger debts and in July he moved to Brighton in order to economize.

Defignd by Helagabalus.  A new way to pay the NATIONAL-DEBT, Dedicated to Monsʳ. Necker.  Executed by Sejanus.

117

### Cheyt Sing in his Eastern Dress

1786

*On 14 June 1786 Warren Hastings, the former governor-general of India, presented the King with a large diamond sent by the Nizam of the Deccan. Its delivery had been delayed so that it arrived a day after the famous debate in the House of Commons on 13 June when Fox and Burke demanded the impeachment of Hastings for the way he had exacted unlawful tribute from Cheit Singh, the Rajah of Benares, and had then deposed him. On 21 June, after news of the gift came out, Sheridan insinuated that it was a bribe for the King. Hastings had also given other gifts to George and Charlotte – the shawl, named in this print, and an ivory bed.*

CHEYT SING
IN HIS EASTERN DRESS.

agreed to an annual allowance from the Civil List of only £50,000 (£3.6 million) although at the same age he had had £100,000 a year. Any hopes that this would lead the Prince to conduct a more frugal way of life were rudely dashed. The debts of the Prince of Wales, £161,000 (£11.5 million) in 1787 and £630,000 (£45 million) in 1795, had to be paid off by Parliament, and his brother, the Duke of York, had to have £54,000 (£3.8 million) cleared during the 1790s. George expressed his concern at their behaviour in a letter to his son William: 'With thirteen children, I can but with the greatest care make both ends meet, and I am not in a situation to be paying their debts, if they contract any, and to anyone that has either the sentiments of common honesty and delicacy, without the nicer feelings which every gentleman ought to possess, the situation of not paying which is due is a very unpleasant situation.'

It was not just George's frugality and his sons' profligacy that were the target of the satirists. Queen Charlotte's supposed avarice and miserliness also came under attack, particulary her acquisition of a vast amount of jewelry. On their marriage, George gave her the Hanoverian hereditary jewels: strings of enormous pearls, a huge number of valuable diamonds – one worth at least £18,000 (£1.3 million) – and the star of the collection, a stomacher of diamonds and pearls valued at £60,000 (£4.3 million). Charlotte was expected to wear these at the Drawing Rooms – palace receptions – and on several occasions she complained to both Fanny Burney and the King about their weight.

As Queen, Charlotte received many gifts, such as the seven large diamonds (subsequently known as the Arcot diamonds) given to her in 1767 by the Nawab of Arcot and she probably took possession of the diamond sent by the Nizam of the Deccan and given to George by Warren Hastings in 1786. Throughout her life Charlotte also bought jewels – the firm of Garrard, subsequently the Crown Jeweller, was kept busy. All her later portraits show her wearing a diamond-encrusted miniature of her husband. The statesman and author John Wilson Croker estimated the value of her jewels at £200,000 (nearly £14 million). The sale of the Queen's effects after her death in 1818 lasted over six days and more than 1,000 pieces of jewelry were sold in 324 lots.

The royal couple's miserly tag was somewhat unfair, at least as far as George was concerned. He was generous in his support of charitable causes – not simply the distribution of the Royal Maundy to poor pensioners every Easter. A committee that examined the Privy Purse after the King's illness in 1789 found

THE QUEEN of HEARTS COVER'D WITH DIAMONDS

Q. Charlotte

## The Queen of Hearts cover'd with Diamonds

1786

*The bulse was the bag that carried the diamond from the Nizam of the Deccan. Charlotte loved diamonds, many of which she inherited and many more that she bought. She wears here a huge earring and takes her favourite pinch of snuff.*

that he gave £14,000 (£1 million) a year to charity from his personal expenditure of £80,000 (£5.7 million). In 1810, to celebrate his jubilee, he gave £6,000 for the relief of poor pensioners and debtors. From the Civil List George allocated just £48,000 (£3.4 million) a year for his household's requirements. The rest was spent on the salaries of judges, civil servants, ambassadors, the Lord Chancellor and the Speaker, as well as a range of other commitments: £5,000 for paving the streets of Westminster; £2,000 for printing the journal of the House of Commons; the board and lodging of court officials (Fanny Burney had a footman and the use of a coach); £1,059 to the Emperor of Morocco to prevent piracy in the Mediterranean; extraordinary payments to MPs, election expenses and rewards for 'special services'; pensions to some and help for others who had fallen on hard times; and finally £50,000 (£3.6 million) was set aside for the secret service.

The only extra cash that George could access was rent from the Duchy of Lancaster and his farms, over £300 (£21,000) a year by 1771. He farmed to make a profit – all those farthings for milk added up. He had to pay for all his personal expenditure on books, the commissioning of royal portraits, his purchase of clocks and scientific instruments, and the Queen's private zoo in St James's Park. The Queen had her own allowance of £40,000 (£2.9 million) a year, but by 1793 her annual expenses were nearly £70,000 (£5 million), even after tight control of her own expenditure and that of their daughters. As she wrote to her brother Charles in about 1783: 'My expenses with five daughters, of whom the oldest appear at Court and are always with us in public, require all the economy imaginable.' It was this parsimony that earned her the reputation of being a grasping skinflint. Her income rose to £100,000 in 1812, but she too soon defaulted and turned to her husband to meet her debts.

The Begging Bow.

Mew mew mew, fal lal &c &c

y S.W. Fores. Nº 3 Piccadilly

## The Bow to the Throne, – alias – The Begging Bow

6 May 1788

JAMES GILLRAY

On 13 February 1788 the impeachment of Warren Hastings began in Westminster Hall. Edmund Burke led the charge: Hastings was accused of 'Avarice, rapacity, pride, insolence, ferocity, treachery, cruelty, malignity of temper.' The case was instigated by the personal jealousy of Sir Philip Francis, who had served in India with Hastings and had been wounded in a duel with him. The impeachment dragged on for several years and Hastings was eventually acquitted in 1795. Burke, Sheridan and Fox were anti-Hastings but Pitt, the Lord Chancellor Thurlow, the King and Queen were seen to be his supporters. Radical prints, sensing that Hastings was going to get off, accused him of bribery, alluding particularly to the large diamond he had given the King in 1786. Although Gillray shows Hastings distributing largesse, he lays the blame on George III who is shown grasping guineas and saying 'I am at the bottom of it'. The first session ended in April 1788 but as the trial rolled on boredom set in and it never again became such a focus of attention.

**Frying Sprats,
Toasting Muffins**

28 November 1791

JAMES GILLRAY

*'Ah! sure a pair was never seen,
So justly formed to meet by nature!'*

*Miserliness, not extravagance, is again Gillray's subject. The Queen as usual is more harshly treated: golden guineas fall from her patched purse. The King's diet was spartan: a small breakfast with tea was followed by a dinner at 4 p.m. with soup, meat – usually mutton – and possibly a pudding of stewed pears. For a treat there would be plover's eggs, cow's heels, or a cherry tart. He preferred barley wine to wine. A simple supper of plain bread and butter or a sandwich was taken after 10 p.m. In the 1790s, the King's bread was either brown or potato bread in order to save cost. Simple and frugal, it was a stark contrast to the gourmet palate of his eldest son.*

**Beauties of a
Gracious
Speech**

2 February 1792

WILLIAM DENT

*In Berlin in September 1791, the Duke of York, George's favourite son, married
Princess Frederica, the eldest daughter of Frederick William II of Prussia. Her
dowry of £30,000 (£2.1 million) was quite modest and could not meet the Duke's
debts, which were largely due to his gambling. Parliament granted him a further
£12,000 and George stumped up as well. Here George urges, 'Settle something on
the poor souls – I would do it with all my Heart – but I am so devilish poor', and
to prove it he is picking up a crooked pin that has been dropped. In the meantime,
John Bull, wearing a fool's cap, shovels guineas into the Yorks' sack. The marriage
was childless and after a few years the couple led separate lives.*

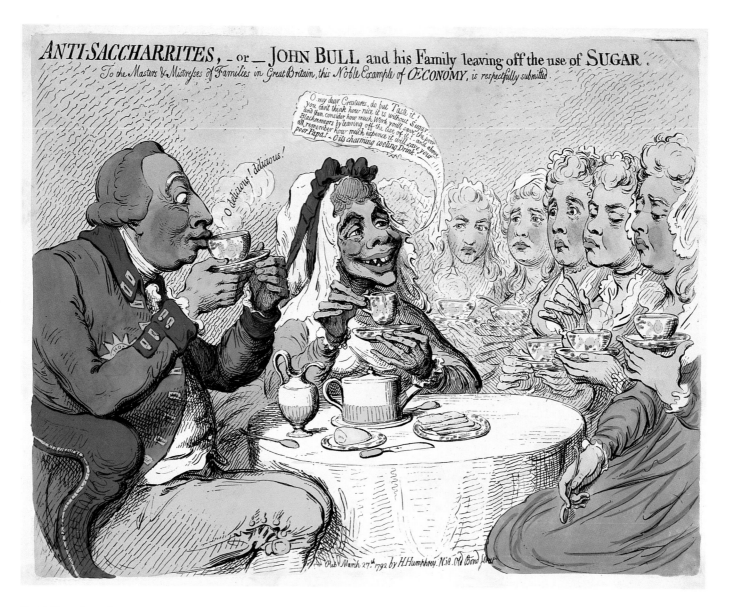

## Anti-Saccharrites, – or – John Bull and his Family leaving off the use of Sugar

27 March 1792

JAMES GILLRAY

Gillray envisages that George and Charlotte have banned sugar from the royal household, much to the dismay of their daughters, led by the Princess Royal on the right, who gloomily and sulkily hold their cups without drinking from them. Charlotte says that abstention from sugar 'will save the poor Blackamoors' from work and 'above all, remember how much expense it will save your poor Papa'. George's abstinence was not due to a desire to alleviate the working conditions in the Caribbean sugar islands for he believed that the slaves were necessary for the prosperity of the Empire. Pitt abandoned Wilberforce's attempts to end the slave trade because 'the King did not approve'. This is one of the more flattering depictions of George but Charlotte's scrawny fingers echo her poor teeth. From 1791 to 1793 Gillray produced some of his most famous cartoons and when George appears in them he is always shown in profile – a device adopted by other caricaturists.

Another attack on the farming activities of the royal couple. 'Come, Come, Give me the money my Bags are not full yet, and I am afraid they never will, you give those Lubbers too much Measure', says Charlotte, greedily reproving George for being too generous in selling his milk, which he has brought in two buckets – even bearing the yoke is not too humble for him. The majesty of monarchy is diminished, as one woman tellingly comments: 'Oh Lord Oh Lord he is nothing but a Man.'

Content and Discontent

21 June 1792

RICHARD NEWTON

*Attacks on George's parsimony reached their peak in 1791–92. This image goes further as it contrasts the prosperity of the Crown and the Church with the cost of food to the poor. A butcher has not sold a joint of meat for a fortnight.*

Temperance enjoying a Frugal Meal

28 July 1792

JAMES GILLRAY

*This is the most famous of the many satires on the King's frugality and the Queen's avarice: George eats an egg and Charlotte a salad. His breeches are patched, his napkin is the tablecloth and his chair is swathed in dustsheets. On the heavily bolted strongroom door behind Charlotte is a 'Table of Interest' listing the returns obtained at a rate of 5 per cent. All the furnishings reflect miserliness: the empty picture frame of* The Triumph of Benevolence; *the empty cornucopias; the half-burnt candles; the flowers in the grate; the balance for weighing guineas; and on the chest a book entitled* Dr Cheyne on the benefits of a Spare Diet. *George was determined not to be as fat as his huge uncles, and between breakfast and dinner, a late afternoon meal, he drank only one cup of tea and never ate anything. Elizabeth, Duchess of Northumberland, who was a Lady of the Bedchamber to Charlotte, described the royal table as 'neither sumptuous nor elegant, and they always dined Tête-à-Tête'.*

TEMPERANCE enjoying a Frugal Meal.

## Royal – Munificence – hem!!!

1 June 1814

CHARLES WILLIAMS

*As a joke, Charlotte's name subscribing 2,000 guineas was added to an appeal for funds to help the Germans, her fellow countrymen, distressed in the war. In this print, she is so startled by this news, as she had given nothing, that she spills her snuff and drops her book,* Frugal Maxims or the Art of Saving. *There are echoes here of Gillray's masterpiece,* Temperance enjoying a Frugal Meal: *the miser's cupboard has sprung open showing bags of cash, farthings and jewels; a tariff of interest rates is on the door; she has only an egg for breakfast while one of her daughters, possibly Sophia, boils up a pan of water. In the picture above her head,* Date Obolum Belisario, *Charlotte is holding a begging bowl and leads her blind husband, in the way the sixth-century general Belisarius, blinded by Justinian, had to beg on the streets. The Queen never shook off her reputation of being stingy and several satires picked up on this in 1813 and 1814. This print appeared in the* Scourge, *a satirical magazine.*

# 9 Murderous Attacks

IN THE COURSE OF George's long life, several attempts were made to kill him, all of which he responded to with coolness, courage and compassion.

The first incident took place on 2 August 1786 when he was alighting from his coach outside St James's Palace to attend a levee. Margaret Nicholson, a former domestic servant, approached him holding a sheet of paper, which he thought was a petition. As George took the paper she lunged clumsily at his chest with 'a large servant's eating-knife with a horn handle, made sharp on both sides', but the blow glanced off his coat. She was quickly seized but the King shouted out, 'the poor creature is mad, do not hurt her. She has not hurt me.' He went on to attend the levee and then returned to Windsor to recount the episode to the Queen and their daughters. 'Here I am safe and well as you see, but I have very narrowly escaped being stabbed.' In spite of George's cheerful composure, they burst into tears. Fanny Burney observed the family's mood: 'In the evening, just as usual, the King had his concert: but it was an evening of grief and horror to his family: nothing was listened to, scarce a word was spoken; the Princesses wept continually; the Queen, still more deeply struck, could only, from time to time hold out her

hand to the King, and say, "I have you yet!"' Burney also noted how the King was greeted with 'loud huzzas' by a crowd at Kew a few days later.

On 21 January 1790, another lunatic, John Frith, threw a rock at George's coach on its way to Parliament. Five years later, on 29 October 1795, at a time of considerable unrest in London owing to a poor harvest, higher taxes and military failures, George was subject to a more menacing attack. On the way to the State Opening of Parliament a large mob cried out 'Peace and Bread! No War! No War! Down with George!' Lord Onslow, a Lord of the Bedchamber who was with the King, recorded what happened next: 'a small ball, either of lead or marble, passed through the window glass on the King's right hand and, perforating it, passed through the coach out of the other door, the glass of which was down. We all instantly exclaimed, "This is a shot!" The King showed…no alarm…."Sit still, my Lord," he rebuked one of his companions who was fidgeting in alarm. "We must not betray fear whatever happens."'

George calmly read his speech to Parliament but on the return journey, as Onslow recorded, the crowd 'of the worst and

AN EXACT REPRESENTATION OF AN ATTEMPT MADE BY MARG.ᵗ NICHOLSON TO STAB HIS MAJESTY ON WEDNESDAY AUG.ᵗ 2 1786

Pub.ᵈ Aug.ᵗ 5 1786 by W.ᵖ Fores at the Caricature Ware-house N.³ 3 Piccadilly

130

## An Exact Representation of an Attempt made by Marg.t Nicholson to Stab His Majesty on Wednesday Aug.t 2 1786

5 August 1786

*This is the first print showing Margaret Nicholson's attempt on the King's life. The event was witnessed by many people and was well recorded. George prevented any violence being shown to her and she was soon confined in the lunatic asylum known as Bedlam, where she spent the remainder of her life writing petitions to the King. George's popularity boosted as news of the attack spread – the nation had come to like its eccentric but decent king, and did not want to see him harmed.*

*A View of the Garden Entrance of St James's Palace.*
*Vûe de l'entrée au Jardin du Palais Royal de St Jaques,*

lowest sort' was even bigger. They 'proceeded to throw stones into the coach [breaking all the glass]. Several stones hit the King, which he bore with signal patience, but not without sensible marks of indignation and resentment at the indignities offered to his person and office....The King took one of the stones out of the cuff of his coat, where it had lodged, and gave it to me saying, "I make you a present of this, as a mark of the civilities we have met with on our journey today".'

In 1800, the King had two lucky escapes, both on the same day, 15 May. In the morning, at a review of the First Foot Guards in Hyde Park, a clerk from the Navy Office who was standing near the King was struck in the leg by a bullet – an accident? Many thought it was meant for George. That evening the King and Queen went to the Theatre Royal, Drury Lane, for a per-

## A View of the Garden Entrance of St James's Palace

1786

ROBERT DIGHTON

*This engraving was published soon after Margaret Nicholson's attack on the King. It was issued by the well-known printseller Carrington Bowles to be sold in England and France. Many of the details are the same as in the print opposite: Yeomen of the Guard are at the door and the would-be assassin has a very large, black hat.*

formance of Colley Cibber's comedy, *She Would and She Would Not*. As the King went forward in the royal box, a man in the pit fired a pistol at him. Michael Kerry, the theatre's musical director, was on stage and saw what happened next: 'The King, on hearing the report of the pistol, retired a pace or two, stopped, and stood firmly for an instant; then came forward to the very front of the box, put his opera-glass to his eye, and looked round the house, without the smallest appearance of alarm or discomposure.' George turned to the Queen: 'We will not stir. We'll stay the entertainment out.' An actress announced that the man had been apprehended and when the audience realized the King was safe they cheered and sang 'God Save the King'. Sheridan, the theatre manager, composed an impromptu extra verse for the national anthem:

From every latent foe,
From the assassin's blow,
   God save the King.
O'er him thine arm extend,
For Britain's sake defend,
Our Father, Prince & Friend,
   God save the King.

James Hadfield, the former soldier who had shot at the King, was tried for high treason but detained as a lunatic in Bedlam for the rest of his life.

In 1802, the Irishman Colonel Edward Despard, a former colonial administrator and shipmate of Horatio Nelson, was arrested for planning to assassinate the King with a view to sparking a republican revolution. Despard and his six accomplices were tried for high treason and were the last men in England sentenced to be hanged, drawn and quartered. In the event, Despard's punishment was changed to a more simple hanging and beheading and he was executed on 21 February 1803.

A Ministerial Fact; or, a Squib of the First Day
Four presumtive Reasons—Because no two Faces in the world are so much alike! Because the Political Proteus was seen in a Mileners shop (where no doubt he bought the Cloak and bonnet) about a month ago! Because he was seen by a Grenadeer of The Guards coming out of a Cutler's shop (where no doubt he bought the knife) yesterday morning! But the strongest reason to suppose him y Assasin is because he was an hundred miles from London at the time !!!
Pub.d by W. Holland. N.66 Drury Lane, Aug.t 2 1786

### A Ministerial Fact; or, a Squib of the First Day

2 August 1786

*The* Gentleman's Magazine *reported that Margaret Nicholson's attack 'circulated through the city with amazing rapidity, and, gathering as it flew, a thousand fictions were added'. Probably one of the 'fictions' was that Fox had something to do with the attack. This caricature, from the anti-ministerial printshop of William Holland, depicts Fox as the would-be assassin in cloak and bonnet, parodying the 'ministerial' caricatures that had wounded him – and clinches the mockery with a comical caption: '...Because the Political Proteus was seen in a Miliner's shop (where no doubt he bought the Cloak and bonnet) about a month ago! Because he was seen by a Grenadier of the Guards coming out of a Cutler's shop (where no doubt he bought the knife) yesterday morning! But the strongest reason to suppose him ye Assassin is because he was an hundred miles from London at the time!!!'*

### Frith the Madman Hurling Treason at the King

31 January 1790

ISAAC CRUIKSHANK

On 21 January 1790, George III was being driven to the opening of Parliament when John Frith, an insane half-pay officer, hurled a large stone into the royal coach. Here Burke, bald and aged (he was now 60), is depicted as Frith, whose arrest dejects Fox, dressed as an old woman, and Sheridan, a sailor, who opines, 'Damn'd unlucky'. These three leaders of the opposition are shown as favouring violence against the Crown just as France descended into turmoil. In the case of Burke, this was not really the case – in February, in a speech to the Commons, he declared his total hostility to the French Revolution. In November, he published Reflections on the Revolution in France, *which helped to turn British public opinion against the revolution.*

C.J Fox.       Burke.       Geo. III.   31 Jan 1790

J.Cruikshanks

FRITH the MADMAN HURLING TREASON. at the KING.

Pub.Jan.31.1790 by S.W.Fores N3 Piccadilly. Where may be seen the Compleatest Collection of Caricatures &c in the Kingdom. Admittance one shilling.

## The Republican Attack

1 November 1795

JAMES GILLRAY

On 29 October 1795, a mob attacked the King's coach on the way to the State Opening of Parliament. Three days later Gillray is depicting Fox, Sheridan and their supporters as the assailants of the King. Pitt is the coachman driving the state coach to safety but, as is so common in Gillray's prints, no one is a hero: Pitt's coach is driving over Britannia, his ministers ride behind as flunkies, the King sits oblivious and the mob are carrying a French flag inscribed with 'Peace and Bread' – the two things the government was not giving them.

Pub.d Nov.r 1.st 1795, by H. Humphrey New Bond Street

The REPUBLICAN-ATTACK.

OUR SOVEREIGN LORD THE KING,
as he appear'd the Moment previous to the DREADFUL mischief intended him
by the Horrid Affaffin James Hadfield at Drury Lane Theatre on Thursd May. 15. 1800.

From ev'ry latent Foe,    "O'er him thine arm extend,    God save
"From the affaffin's blow,    "For Britain's sake defend,    the KING.
"God fave the KING.    "Our Father, Prince, & Friend,

## Our Sovereign Lord the King

19 May 1800

ROBERT DIGHTON

*Dighton depicts the scene at the Drury Lane Theatre when George kept his calm after an assassination attempt and came forward to the front of his box, placing his opera-glass to his eye. The audience roared their support for his sang-froid and his survival. Sheridan's new verse for the national anthem, commemorating the occasion, is printed below the image.*

## Britannias Protection or Loyalty Triumphant

4 June 1800

THOMAS ROWLANDSON

*George calmly rests on the pillar of fortitude, protected by Britannia and her spear. James Hadfield, the madman who shot at the King in the Drury Lane Theatre, is led away by a demon saying, 'For thy diabolical attempt thou shall meet with thy reward.' Hadfield ended up in Bedlam.*

BRITANNIAS PROTECTION OR LOYALTY TRIUMPHANT.

# 10 The Patron

## Music

George's great love was music. He said to Fanny Burney at their first meeting: 'To me it appears quite as strange to meet with people who have no ear for music and cannot distinguish one air from another as to meet with people who are dumb.' In 1788, the Princess Royal wrote that 'a love of music to distraction runs through our family,' but added, 'of which I alone am deprived.' The King played the flute, the violin and the harpsichord, which gave him considerable enjoyment in his final lonely, senile years.

Throughout his life George showed his devotion to Handel, who had died in 1759: a bust by Roubiliac of the composer was placed in an honoured position in Buckingham House; and the King was proud to own a harpsichord that had once been Handel's. When Johann Christian Bach, the youngest son of J. S. Bach, settled in London in 1762 – he was called 'the English Bach' – he was soon appointed Music Master to Queen Charlotte, and in 1764 the royal couple welcomed the eight-year-old prodigy Mozart. The King and Queen's attendance at programmes arranged by the Concert of Ancient Music, which had been founded in 1776, was so frequent that they became known as the King's Concerts. George was on the committee that chose the programme and Handel's music featured prominently. Handel had been right when he had said of George: 'While that boy lives my music will never want a protector.'

W. Hogarth inv.º et del.　　　　　　　C. Grignion sculp.

*Et spes & ratio Studiorum in Cæsare tantum.*

Juv.

Published according to Act of Parliament May 7, 1761.

## Frontispiece to the Artist's Catalogue

1761

WILLIAM HOGARTH

*This was the front of a catalogue from an exhibition of paintings held to benefit distressed artists and their families. When Hogarth was recognized as the artist there was a run on the catalogue, which also served as an admission ticket. The Latin motto declares: 'The hopes and rewards of learning depend upon Caesar.'*

*From a monument bearing George's bust a stream of water gushes out and is directed by Britannia's watering can on to the three saplings of 'Painting', 'Sculpture' and 'Architecture'. One year into the reign, this shows that there were high hopes the young King would support the arts; it was known already that with Bute's guidance he had bought paintings and books. In the following ten years he was to purchase two major collections of paintings and quadruple the size of his library.*

## Odes for the New Year, 1787

1787

THOMAS ROWLANDSON

*The satirical verses of Peter Pindar (the pen name of John Wolcot, chosen perhaps because of the ancient Greek poet Pindar's reputation for belonging to no faction) were published in the morning and evening newspapers and in pamphlets for over twenty years. This print accompanied an edition of Peter Pindar's odes. Both George III and Peter Pindar are thrown off Pegasus, the winged horse and inspiration of poetry, by a harlequin who represents satire. In the classical story, Bellerophon attempted to fly on Pegasus to the heights of Mount Olympus but Zeus was so angered at the presumption that he sent an insect to torment Pegasus, causing Bellerophon to fall. Clearly Pindar's odes were hitting home.*

## Books

Lord Bute encouraged George's interest in books before he ascended the throne and he appointed the Prince's first librarian in 1755. George started to amass a library that grew to 65,000 volumes and 450 manuscripts; it was presented by George IV to the British Museum and is now part of the British Library. The collection included music books from the library of the composer William Boyce; a Gutenberg Bible; several books printed by Caxton; Shakespeare folios; a first edition of *Paradise Lost*; and many works by 18th-century writers – the King's favourites were Henry Fielding and Dr Johnson.

In 1762, George bought the library of George Thomason, a 17th-century London bookseller who had amassed a great collection of pamphlets, tracts and newspapers, chiefly relating to the Civil War. In the same year Bute helped him to acquire the magnificent library of Joseph Smith, the British consul in Venice, who had been collecting for over thirty years. Four library rooms were added to Buckingham House to accommodate these collections and they were open for use by scholars.

Throughout his life, George paid for his books from his own private resources, spending up to £2,000 (£140,000) a year. He was also interested in the external appearance of his books and established a royal bindery in five basement rooms of Buckingham House. A poem of 1796 chided him for being more interested in the appearance of books than their contents:

> And yet our Monarch has a world of books,
> And daily on their backs so gorgeous looks;
> So neatly bound, so richly gilt, so fine,
> He fears to open them to read a line!

George also amassed a vast number of atlases and topographical views. These seemed to quench his insatiable curiosity about places that he would never see, since he found the prospect of overseas travel too disruptive. His furthest excursions were to Cheltenham and Weymouth: in the fifty years of his active reign he never ventured beyond England. He became the best-informed armchair traveller in the world.

## Paintings

Like so much else, George's taste in paintings was guided by Bute; it was Bute's younger brother who in 1762 acquired for the

King the outstanding collection of the consul Joseph Smith for £20,000 (£1.4 million). As well as the library, this added five hundred canvasses by such Italian masters as Zuccarelli, Longhi and the Ricci, and an unrivalled collection of 50 paintings and 143 drawings by Canaletto; also a number of north European paintings including Vermeer's exquisite masterpiece – *Lady at the Virginal*. In the same year, Bute orchestrated the acquisition of the collection of prints and drawings of Cardinal Alessandro Albani, which included drawings by Domenichino, Poussin and the Carracci.

George bought these because he was advised to do so. He did not, unlike his son, the Prince Regent, become a connoisseur, collecting a wide range of paintings because he personally liked them. After 1770, when the influence of Bute had faded, he did not add any significant Old Master works to the royal collection. He preferred the work of his contemporary, the American-born artist Benjamin West, from whom he acquired some sixty pictures between 1768 and 1801 – large dramatic paintings with ennobling messages: classical, religious and historic. George liked pictures that told a story.

The King also loved portraits and when still Prince of Wales he was introduced by Bute to the Scottish artist Allan Ramsay, who became the King's Principal Painter at the accession. But George's favourite artist was Thomas Gainsborough, who enjoyed 'talking bawdy to the King and morality to the Prince of Wales'. George also enjoyed the very literal portrayals of the royal family by the German-born Johan Zoffany. Portraiture was a way in which the power, significance, grandeur and supremacy of the Crown could be established, reinforced and made evident to the world.

## Porcelain

Josiah Wedgwood was styled 'Potter to Her Majesty' from 1766 after making a tea service for Charlotte in a design that became known as Queen's Ware. George took a great interest in the manufacturing process and invited Wedgwood to Windsor to discuss the industry.

## Clocks, Scientific Instruments and Astronomy

George was fascinated by all kinds of scientific instruments, including barometers, microscopes, timepieces and orreries. His interest in the precision and minutiae of complex mechanisms was another aspect of his passionate devotion to detail. He bought clocks from the two leading clockmakers – Alexander Cumming and Christopher Pinchbeck, and paid Cumming

Pubd May 10th 1787, by S.W.Ford, Piccadilly.

*ANCIEN*

Monarchs, who, with Rapture wild,
Hear their own Praise with Mouths, of gaping Wonder,
And catch each Crotchet of the Birth-day Thunder. Peter Pindar.

USIC.

## Ancient Music

10 May 1787

JAMES GILLRAY

By 1785 the King and Queen were attending the programmes of the Concert of Ancient Music. The music had to be at least twenty years old and George, as one of the directors, helped to select the pieces, often including those of his great favourite, Handel. This print, in part criticising the King's old-fashioned taste, was based upon a satire by Peter Pindar that attacked the obsequiousness of the audiences. A verse from Pindar's Ode upon Ode beneath the print reads:

— Monarchs, who with Rapture
  wild,
Hear their own Praise with
Mouths of gaping Wonder,
And catch each Crotchet of the
Birth-day Thunder.

George is depicted in a state of ecstasy brought on by the cacophony of the 'orchestra' of sycophants. The front row consists of directors of the Concert of Ancient Music (Joah Bates, its founder, is an ox). At the top is Thurlow, the Lord Chancellor, who is flogging boys. Pitt, to the King's right, is blowing a penny whistle and three royal hounds chase Fox whose tail carries a pot with the face of North. The parsimony of the King and Queen, who attended the concerts at other people's houses rather than in their own palace, is emphasized by the imp holding two purses atop the canopy. This is the first impression of this print. The second shows stubble on the Queen's face and her nose dripping.

## Portraits of their Majesty's and the Royal Family

1788 (susequently made into a fan)

PIETRO MARTINI AFTER RAMBERG

*When George learnt in 1768 that several artists were proposing a 'School or Academy of Design, for the use of students in the Arts, and an annual exhibition, open to all artists of distinguished merit', he supported it with enthusiasm, helping to draw up its Instrument of Foundation, which he signed. He contributed £5,000 (£358,000) to the initial cost of the Royal Academy of Arts and was given the right to nominate Royal Academicians. Joshua Reynolds, not the King's favourite painter, became the first president. The Academy's significance as a national cultural institution was recognized by its move to the rebuilt Somerset House in 1780, and it became the first artistic body to be housed at public expense. Art was an important contribution to a nation's glory.*

£1,178 (£84,000) for a magnificent barograph – a mechanical device that recorded changes in atmospheric pressure. He also liked using tools himself: he kept a precise record of how to assemble a watch and at Windsor he installed a lathe and turned out some buttons – an accomplishment that was seized upon by the caricaturists.

George's interest in astronomy stemmed from one of his tutors, Stephen Demainbray; in 1768 he appointed him keeper of the new royal observatory at Kew and in 1769 he watched the transit of Venus there. George supported the astronomer William Herschel, who had had a chequered career as a musician and organist before he became a self-taught astronomer. In 1781, he discovered the planet Uranus and initially named it *Georgium sidus* in honour of the King. Herschel was granted £2,000 (£140,000) in 1785 and £4,000 (£280,000) in 1787 to construct a giant forty-foot telescope at Slough, close enough to Windsor for George to visit and study the galaxies.

### Peter's Pension

1788

THOMAS ROWLANDSON

*Peter Pindar (John Wolcot) attacked Pitt, his ministers and Royal Academicians, but his favourites were George and Charlotte. Every week there were witty gibes about the couple's parsimony, the Hastings diamond, Farmer George, the use of man-traps on the King's farms, his debts, and his blustering manner of questioning all and sundry. Rowlandson depicts the King attempting to bribe Pindar – which had happened in 1785 when he was given an advance of £300 from the Treasury but he returned it before he wrote anything further. One of his poems described the dilemma:*

> *This pension was well meant, Oh Glorious King,*
> *And for the bard a very pretty thing;*
> *But let me, Sir refuse it, I implore –*
> *I ought not to be rich whilst you are poor;*
> *No, Sir I cannot be your humble hack;*
> *I fear your Majesty would break my back.*

### A Sketch from High Life

27 May 1791

RICHARD NEWTON

*George loved and understood portraiture but he would have preferred to have been painted by Zoffany than caricatured by the young Richard Newton – this was his first recorded print. Newton kept the same image of George for the next seven years of his short life.*

*Representation of a Royal Concert, at Buckingham House*

## Representation of a Royal Concert, at Buckingham House

1792

INIGO BARLOW AFTER ISAAC CRUIKSHANK

*At this concert in Buckingham House three of George's daughters, Charlotte, the Princess Royal, with a mandolin, Princess Augusta at the piano and Princess Elizabeth with the song-sheet, regale their parents and their younger sister Amelia. The two young men could be the Prince of Wales and the Duke of York. The violinist is one of the musicians employed to teach the royal family. Music was important to the King and Queen, but the only one of their children who was musically gifted was the Prince of Wales, who played the cello and had a fine singing voice.*

## Mr Follet as the Clown in the Pantomime of Harlequin and Oberon

3 April 1797

RICHARD NEWTON

*By royal command, John Follet, the leading clown of the day, plays the lead in a farce at Covent Garden. Not a scholar, George's taste was more that of a well-read country squire. He did not care much for Shakespeare, telling Fanny Burney that it was 'sad stuff....Only one must not say so! What?–What?'*

MR FOLLET AS THE CLOWN IN THE PANTOMIME OF HARLEQUIN AND OBERON

## Consistancy!! – or Rival Clowns in the new Pantomime of *Harlequin & Quixote*

8 January 1798

RICHARD NEWTON

*This disrespectful portrayal of George, by the young radical caricaturist Richard Newton, shows the King as one clown staring at another – Don Quixote. George and Charlotte were enthusiastic theatre-goers – attending regularly but with a preference for 'good modern comedies'. Harlequin & Quixote had been playing at Drury Lane for two years and John Follet (on the right), the famous clown of the day and a favourite of the King, was the star.*

### Self-portrait of Richard Newton holding his print of Mr Follet

*This watercolour is the only known likeness of the young artist Richard Newton. He died in 1798 at the age of twenty-one, possibly from jail fever picked up on his visits to the inmates of Newgate prison – radical publishers and booksellers, including for a time his own publisher, William Holland, who was serving a sentence for publishing pamphlets supporting Tom Paine's* Rights of Man. *Newton's talent was unique – quite distinct from Rowlandson and Gillray. He was neglected by the Victorians but has been rediscovered in the last twenty years.*

# 11 France and Revolution

IN HIS BUDGET SPEECH on 17 February 1792 Pitt made a fatal forecast: 'There never was a time in the history of this country when, from the situation of Europe, we might more reasonably expect fifteen years of peace than we may at the present moment.'

Eight weeks later, on 20 April, France declared war on Austria, which was soon joined by Prussia. In May, Catherine II of Russia invaded Poland, also aided by Prussia, which wanted part of the spoils. The Duke of Brunswick (George's brother-in-law), leading the Austrian and Prussian forces invading France, issued a proclamation promising Paris 'military execution and total subversion' if the royal family was harmed; this galvanized the republican fervour of the French. On 10 August, a mob stormed the Tuileries, where the royal family was confined, and the monarchy was suspended. In early September, frenzied mobs invaded the Parisian jails and brutally murdered over 1,000 prisoners. Europe was horrified by the turn of events. In the field, the French army, marching to the 'Marseillaise', crushed Brunswick's army at Valmy on 20 September. The next day, the National Convention voted to establish a republic and proceeded to try the King for treason.

Pitt acted swiftly to curb radicals at home and to fight the revolutionaries in France. Parliament was recalled to sanction the calling out of the militia in several counties. Thomas Paine, an elected member of the French National Convention, who wrote *The Rights of Man* as a riposte to Burke's *Reflections on*

THE TELL TALE IN HIGH CREDIT WITH THE STATE GOSSIPS.

### The Tell Tale in High Credit with the State Gossips

8 January 1791

WILLIAM DENT

*The publication of Edmund Burke's* Reflections on the Revolution in France *in November 1790 gave intellectual stuffing to those who were alarmed at what was happening across the Channel. Hitherto there had been much sympathy for the revolution, which Fox called 'one of the most glorious events in the history of mankind'. Burke disagreed, abandoned the Whigs and supported Pitt. Here the King is prepared to overlook Burke's earlier attacks upon the power of the Crown and has invited him to tea. Dent was pro-Whig and anti-monarch. He attacked Burke's apostasy and shows Pitt offering Burke a coronet. In 1794, Burke accepted a pension from the King, for which the Whigs criticized him.*

FRENCH DEMOCRATS *surprizing the Royal Runaways.*

Pub June 27th 1791 by
H. Humphrey N.18 Old Bond Street

the Revolution in France, was tried *in absentia* for seditious libel. An Aliens Bill was introduced in December to regulate the movement of foreigners, particularly French refugees.

In 1789 and 1790 George may well have regarded the French Revolution as a divine punishment upon France for supporting the American rebels, but as it became more radical and regicidal George knew that war was necessary 'for the preservation of society'. In January 1793, news came of the execution of Louis XVI and on 1 February France declared war on Britain and Holland. From then on Pitt and George were coupled as the leaders of a free Britain against an enslaved France. The war, with a brief break, lasted for the rest of George's active reign.

### French Democrats surprizing the Royal Runaways

27 June 1791

JAMES GILLRAY

*In June 1791, Louis XVI, Marie Antoinette and their children fled Paris, but on being recognized at Varennes they were taken back and imprisoned. Gillray feared the breakdown of order that the revolution would bring in its wake – his democrats are murderers and ruffians. One of the reasons for George's growing popularity was that living in an age where anarchy and terror were ever-present threats, he represented civility, security and the proper order of things.*

## The Hopes of the Party, prior to July 14th. –
## 'From such wicked Crown & Anchor Dreams, good Lord, deliver us.'

19 July 1791

JAMES GILLRAY

*Radicals Whigs met at the Crown and Anchor in the Strand on 14 July for a dinner to celebrate the second anniversary of the taking of the Bastille. Fox and Sheridan prudently did not attend but Gillray dares to depict them executing the King: Fox is wielding the axe and Sheridan steadies George's head. They are supported on the left by the radical politician John Horne Tooke in a very suggestive pose and on the right by Sir Cecil Wray, an MP who was the steward at the dinner. The man leaning over Sheridan is Joseph Priestley, the dissenting minister and noted scientist, whose association with a similar 14 July dinner in Birmingham stirred up three days of rioting by 'Church and King' agitators, in which Priestley's house was sacked and his library and laboratory were destroyed. To the cheers of the crowd Pitt and Charlotte are strung up on lamp brackets. Gillray cannot resist a sexual allusion – Pitt appears to be pleasuring the Queen. George is simply baffled, not understanding his predicament: 'What! What! What! What's the matter now?' By this time, Gillray had become thoroughly alarmed about the French Revolution and produced a series of prints depicting its horrors. He became one of the bulwarks of the constitution and the Crown, and although Gillray depicts George with a large arse, he is nevertheless the victim. The King is no longer a figure of fun – he is the head of the nation who must be saved. From now on Gillray depicts the King always in profile with the craziness suppressed.*

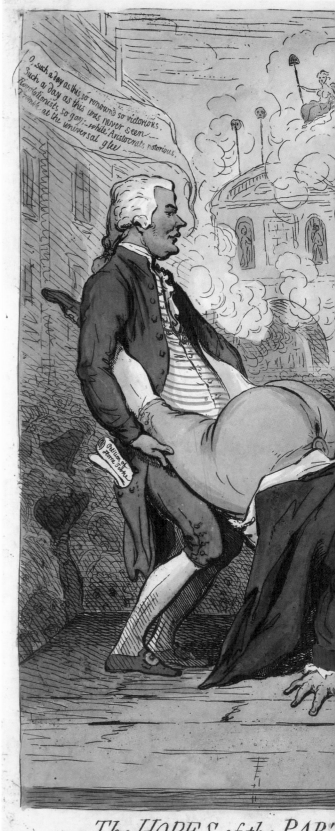

The HOPES of the PART

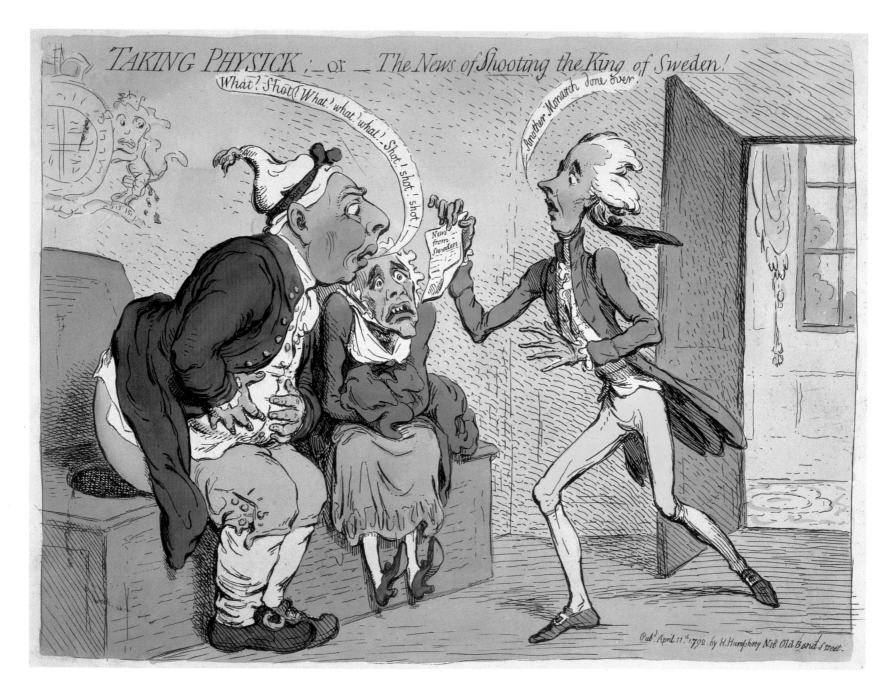

**Taking Physick: – or – The News of Shooting the King of Sweden!**

11 April 1792

JAMES GILLRAY

In March 1792, Europe began to slide into the abyss. Leopold II of Austria died suddenly and was succeeded by the more hard-line Francis II; the Girondins, who advocated continental war, took over in Paris, and Gustavus III of Sweden was shot in the Stockholm Opera House. An alarmed Pitt brings the news to the King and Queen in their privy: 'What! Shot! What! What! What! Shot! Shot! Shot!', says the King. A rare and early glimpse of the royal bottom. On 20 April the French declared war on Austria – the French Revolutionary Wars had begun.

## Louis dethron'd: or Hell broke loose in Paris!!!

16 August 1792

RICHARD NEWTON

*On 10 August, after early reverses in the war with Austria and Prussia, and rumours of treason by the King, mobs stormed the Tuileries, where the royal family was held, slaughtering 600 members of the Swiss Guard. The Legislative Assembly suspended the monarchy. Here George is very alarmed by the news Pitt brings of the French 'Hell Hounds': 'The infernal yell sounds in my ears this moment!' Charlotte, claiming that she knew it would happen, grabs £200,000 and prepares to bolt.*

## Liberty & Equality

20 November 1792

RICHARD NEWTON

*Newton was only fifteen when he drew this caricature depicting George and Charlotte embracing radical ways. Charlotte is drinking with a market woman in one of the worst slums of London, St Giles, and George is walking arm-in-arm with a working man carrying Paine's* Rights of Man. *To complete the miracle, the Lord Chamberlain rides on an ass and a corpulent vicar shares his dinner with a young curate. Newton knew this was a fantasy – but if only…!!*

## The Tree of Liberty, or, European Alarm

*c.* 1792–93

WILLIAM DENT

*The crowned heads of Europe are in a state of alarm bordering upon despair about the flourishing tree of revolutionary republicanism, which is surmounted by the cap of liberty and watered by a bewigged Frenchman. Most of the monarchs are at a loss what to do, apart from Catherine of Russia who is confident that she can freeze them to death. George's comment is, 'What, what, what a Tree! How it branches out! why it's Root will spread all over Europe if it is not Grub'd up.' However, none of the monarchs appeared capable of doing that.*

## The Blood of the Murdered crying for Vengeance

16 February 1793

JAMES GILLRAY

*The radical Gillray was appalled by the excesses of the French Revolution – news of Louis XVI's execution had reached England at the end of January. In this simple and rather crude print the King's decapitated head urges Britain to 'revenge the blood of a Monarch most undeservedly butchered and rescue the Kingdom of France from being the prey of Violence, Usurpation & Cruelty'. Gillray uses this shocking image to warn the people that such an event might well happen in Britain. All Europe was chilled by Danton's declaration that France had thrown down its gauntlet to the kings of Europe, and that gauntlet was the head of a king.*

Published by J. Aitken Castle Street Leicester Square
Oct. 1. 1796

## Prepared for a French Invasion

1 October 1796

WILLIAM O'KEEFE

In July 1796, the French revolutionary government, now in the hands of the Directory, had decided to invade Ireland as an extension of the war against Britain, encouraged by those seeking an independent Irish republic. This print by the Irish engraver William O'Keefe shows George and Pitt determined to hold off an invasion by French devils, one of them holding up a model guillotine. The King and Pitt are supported by an army of armed harridans, some shooting, others vomiting, screaming and praying. The large French fleet emphasizes the danger to England. On 16 October Pitt proposed a supplementary militia of 60,000, which Fox strongly opposed as he believed the threat was a false alarm. In December, a large French invasion fleet was scattered and suffered heavy losses in a howling gale off Bantry Bay in County Cork – the weather was Britain's ally.

**Vent Contraire ou Vaillans efforts du Beau Sexe Anglais pour empêcher la descente [Contrary Wind or Valiant efforts of the English fair sex to prevent the invasion]**

1803

*After the brief peace secured by the Treaty of Amiens in 1802, England declared war on France in May 1803 and Napoleon prepared to invade England. This rare French satire scorns the English war effort. Englishwomen, mostly fat, meagre or ugly, desperately flap their fans to prevent a French invasion fleet from landing. One of them tells George to hide and he replies, 'I am lost.'*

**Mieux vaut tard que jamais! [Better late than never!]**

c. 1807

*By mid-1807 the French were in the ascendancy: the Austrians had withdrawn from the coalition and the Russians had been routed at Friedland. Tsar Alexander I is made to spew up various territories and this French print hopes that George will follow suit by surrendering Malta, Ceylon and Pondicherry – misplaced optimism. Frederick Willliam III of Prussia, now a French vassal, stands in a corner and says he has nothing more to give.*

# 12 Farmer George

GEORGE AND CHARLOTTE had decided that Windsor was 'just the place for us' and as the castle had been neglected since 1714 they asked Sir William Chambers to design them a new house. Windsor became the family home and they moved into Queen's Lodge during the summer of 1778. The sons were found apartments in the castle and the younger daughters lived in an adjacent house, the Lower Lodge.

George's interest in agriculture and stock-breeding had been aroused by the Earl of Bute, who was a scholarly botanist. By the mid-1780s George was farming the small park at Windsor, but it was not until he took over the Rangership of the Great Park when his brother the Duke of Cumberland died in 1790 that he started to farm in earnest, creating three farms, and this accounts for a spate of caricatures in the early 1790s.

### Farmer G——e, Studying the Wind & Weather

1 October 1771

*OXFORD MAGAZINE*

*This is the first reference to George as a farmer. The magazine chides him for neglecting his farm and his flock 'while he is observing the fickleness of the wind or making a curious button and a twopenny snuffbox'. His hobby of making buttons and other small objects was a subject of derision. He holds his telescope the wrong way round. A dog sits on the torn remains of 'the Remonstrance' – one of many political protests from the City. In the background looms Lord Bute with his hand next to the crown.*

*Farmer G—e, Studying the Wind & Weather.*

### Farmer George & his Wife

1785

*An early print of Farmer George.*

## Going To Market

21 November 1791

*Farmer George in a two-wheeled farm cart is off to market with Charlotte as a market woman carrying a basket of cocks and hens on her lap. She receives advice from her husband, 'This cock is very troublesome Charley; shift the basket about.' He goes on to sing one of Tom D'Urfey's songs:*

> *When the Kine had giv'n a pail full,*
> *And the Sheep came bleating home;*
> *Doll, who knew it would be healthful,*
> *Went a walking with young Tom;*
> *Hand in hand, Sir, o'er the land, Sir,*
> *As they walked to and fro;*
> *Tom made jolly love to Dolly,*
> *But was answer'd no, no, no, no, Tom,*
> *no Tom, no Tom, no! &c*

*During his illness George often sang merry songs and catches. This one ends with Doll singing, 'Ay ay ay, ay ay ay, ay ayay'.*

## The Thieves detected at last, or, a Wonderful discovery at the Windsor Farm!!

8 November 1792

RICHARD NEWTON

*Farmer George and his wife are simple country folk happy to find that the geese, not the milkmaids, are stealing the milk. Although absurd, this must have been gossip, which also inspired Peter Pindar:*

> *Of kings who pride themselves on*
> *fruitful sows;*
> *Who sell skim milk and keep a guard so*
> *stout*
> *To drive the geese, the thievish rascals,*
> *out,*
> *That ev'ry morning us'd to suck the*
> *cows.*

GOING TO MARKET.

The Thieves detected at last . or, a Wonderful discovery at the Windsor Farm!!

The Pig brought to a bad Market.
A Fruitless
"Please your Ma...tys. reverence there
"is not a prettier pig in the market.
"Dont impose upon me Dick - it wont do -
" wont do I tell you - what, what, do you think
" I cant see - a very great blemish Dick - got but
" one eye !!
Depend upon it I will
requite you - try what you
can do for me in the upper
house.
Woodward delin

## The Pig brought to a bad Market

GEORGE MOUTARD WOODWARD

*This watercolour by 'Mustard George' relates George's poor eyesight to the same weakness in the pig. The pig's owner claims that it is the prettiest in the market but George, using his spyglass, claims it has only one eye.*

## 'Birthday Ode' (an extract)

1787

PETER PINDAR

*Peter Pindar, the satiric versifier, picked upon the King's visit in May 1787 to Whitbread's London brewery to poke fun at his repetitive staccato way of speaking and his muddle over hay, grain, hops and malt, and his pride in his pigs.*

To Whitbread now deign'd Majesty to say,
'Whitbread, are all your Horses fond of Hay?'
'Yes, please your Majesty,' in humble notes
The Brewer answer'd: 'also, Sir, of Oats.
Another thing my Horses too maintains;
And that, an't please your Majesty, are Grains.'

'Grains, grains,' said Majesty, 'to fill their crops?
Grains, grains? That comes from hops; yes, hops,
hops, hops.'

Here was the King, like Hounds sometimes, at fault.
'Sire,' cried the humble Brewer, 'give me leave
Your sacred Majesty to undeceive:
Grains, Sire, are never made from Hops, but Malt.'

'True,' said the cautious Monarch with a smile:
'From malt, malt, malt: I meant malt all the while.'–
'Yes,' with the sweetest bow rejoined the Brewer,
'An't please your Majesty, you did, I'm sure.'–
'Yes,' answered Majesty with quick reply,
'I did, I did, I did, I, I, I, I.'...

And now before their Sovereign's curious eye,
Parents and Children, fine fat hopeful sprigs,
All snuffing, squinting, grunting, in their sty,
Appear'd the Brewer's tribe of handsome Pigs:
On which th'observant Man who fills a Throne,
Declared the Pigs were vastly like his own:

On which the Brewer, swallowed up in joys,
Tears and astonishment in both his eyes,
His soul brimful of sentiments so loyal,
Exclaimed: 'O Heavens! and can my Swine
Be deemed by Majesty so fine?
Heavens! can my Pigs compare, Sire, with Pigs Royal?'
To which the King assented with a nod:
On which the Brewer bowed, and said, 'Good God!'
Then wink'd significant on Miss,
Significant of wonder and of bliss;
Who, bridling in her chin divine,
Cross'd her fair hands, a dear old Maid,
And then her lowest curtsey made
For such high honour done her Father's Swine.

## AGRICULTURE. 65

### ON MR. DUCKET's MODE OF CULTIVATION.

*By Mr. Ralph Robinson, of Windsor.*

*January 1, 1787.*

S I R,

IT is reasonable to expect that your laudable efforts for the improvement of husbandry, by publishing the Annals of Agriculture, must in time be crowned with success; therefore it seems incumbent on all who think they have materials on this interesting subject worthy of the inspection of the public, to transmit them to you, who, if you view them in that light, will give them a place in that estimable work.

Without further preface, I shall mention that the dispute which has lately arisen on the subject of summer fallows, had made me secretly wish that Mr. Ducket, the able cultivator of Petersham, in Surrey, would have communicated his thoughts, not only on that subject, but would have benefited the public, by a full explanation of that course of husbandry which has rendered his farm at Petersham, which has now been above nineteen years in his hands so flourishing, though his three predecessors had failed on it.

When he first entered on it, all the land, except the meadows, appeared to be hungry sand,

VOL. VII. No. 37.　　E　　and

### Farmer LOOBY manuring the Land.

1794

IS LOOBY only fit
To dung the verdant plain?
Yes, LOOBY has got wit
To fack the golden grain.

*A TOAST.*

MAY every Tyrant fall from power and state;
To be made Ploughmen quickly be their fate;
But that some care of these fine Lads be taken,
May KATE be made to boil their broth and bacon.

**George, the secret Windsor journalist**

January 1787

*An example of George using the pseudonym Ralph Robinson to write to Arthur Young's* Annals of Agriculture *regretting that a Mr Ducket of Petersham had not passed on his tips about the rotation of fallow crops, clover and turnips with wheat, barley and oats.*

**Farmer Looby manuring the Land**

1794

*This crude woodcut with republican verses probably sold for a penny or less.*

## Affability

10 February 1795

JAMES GILLRAY

*George enjoyed walking around his farms, meeting his workers, and entering their cottages unannounced. This startled yokel is getting the full treatment: he is overpowered by the King thrusting his face close to his and blurting out a battery of staccato questions – 'Well, Friend, where a'you going, Hay? – what's your Name, hay? – where d'ye Live, hay? – hay?' The yokel's bucket is full of pigs' offal.*

AFFABILITY.

"Well, Friend, where a'you going, Hay? — what's your Name, hay? — where d'ye Live, hay? — hay?"

## Learning to Make Apple Dumplings

27 November 1797

RICHARD NEWTON

*This is an illustration to* The Apple Dumplings and the King *in Peter Pindar's* An Apologetic Postscript to Ode upon Ode.

> *Enter'd, through curiosity, a cot,*
> *Where sat a poor old woman and her pot.*
>        . . . . .
> *In tempting row the naked dumplings lay,*
> *When, lo! the Monarch, in his usual way,*
> *Like lightning spoke, What's this? What's this?*
>     *What? What?*
>        . . . . .
> *Very astonishing indeed! – Strange thing! –*
> *(Turning the dumpling round, rejoin'd the King),*
> *Tis most extraordinary then, all this is –*
> *It beats Pinetti's conjuring all to pieces –*
> *Strange I should never of a dumpling dream –*
> *But goody, tell me where, where, where's the seam?*
>
> *Sir, there's no seam, quoth she; I never knew*
> *That folks did apple dumplings sew –*
> *No! cry'd the staring Monarch with a grin,*
> *How, how the devil got the apple in?*

LEARNING to MAKE APPLE DUMPLINGS

At Richmond George put sheep in the Old Deer Park and on the advice of Sir Joseph Banks he bought sheep from Spain and became involved in breeding the ancestors of the merino sheep that were to go to Australia and New Zealand.

He amassed a large collection of books on husbandry, many annotated with his own notes, which clearly show a lively and professional interest: 'If the hay is stained by showery weather in making, mixing a peck of salt with a ton of hay will make the cattle feed upon it.' George read *The Annals of Agriculture* from its inception in 1784 and even contributed two letters in 1787 under the pseudonym Ralph Robinson, the name of one of his shepherds. The editor was the agriculturalist Arthur Young, and after he had accompanied George on a tour of the farms he wrote: 'the strong land farm is in admirable order, and the crops all clean and fine.'

George enjoyed dropping in totally unannounced to the cottages of his farm workers. Charles Knight, the Windsor bookseller, noted, 'He had an extraordinary facility for recognizing everybody, young or old.' On one occasion he came across a boy in the Great Park and asked him, 'Who are you?' 'I be pig boy but I don't work. They don't want lads here. All this belongs hereabouts to Georgy.' 'Pray, who is Georgy?' 'He is King and lives at the Castle, but he does no good to me.' The King found a job for him on one of the farms.

It is easy to mock Farmer George but farming was the main occupation of his subjects, many of whom must have been rather proud that their king knew so much about their way of life and spent many happy hours on his farms.

> Let great George his porkers bilk,
> And give his maids the sour skim-milk;
> With her stores let CERES crown him,
> Till the gracious sweat run down him,
> Making butter night and day:
> Well! Well!
> Every king must have his way;
> But to my poor way of thinking,
> True joy is drinking.

## A Visit to the Irish Pig!! with reflections Physical & Moral

7 January 1799

ISAAC CRUIKSHANK

*After the Irish rebellion of 1798, a Mr Wright of Wicklow brought to George at Windsor as a peace offering a huge pig, the Enniscorthy boar, which the print says was five feet high and ten feet long. George welcomes it with 'True – true – very fat – very fat Ireland!' An Irishman from Wexford joked that it was so large because it had eaten Protestant clergymen of Enniscorthy after the battle. When George heard this he ordered the pig to be sold. A contemporary record reveals that after the rebellion 'there was no sale for bacon cured in Ireland, from the well-founded dread of the hogs having fed upon the flesh of men'.*

# 13 God Save the King

BRITAIN AND FRANCE were at war for thirty of the sixty years of George's reign. Battles were fought in Europe, North Africa, India, North America and the West Indies. When Britain was faced with domestic and overseas threats, patriotism flourished: in 1740, 'Rule Britannia' by James Thomson, a Scot, was set to music by Thomas Arne and as Bonnie Prince Charlie marched towards London in 1745 'God Save the King' was sung for the first time in a London theatre. By 1800 it had become the national anthem – a phrase, incidentally, that the British invented.

During this period a huge army and navy were built up; Britain established and maintained its supremacy through the force of arms. In 1789, the army numbered 40,000, but by the end of the Napoleonic Wars in 1815 it was 250,000 strong;

ARMING in the DEFENCE of the FRENCH PRINCES or the PARTING of HECTOR and ANDROMACHE.

## Arming in the Defence of the French Princes or the Parting of Hector and Andromache

8 May 1792

RICHARD NEWTON

*On 20 April, just over two weeks before this print appeared, France had declared war on Austria. A week later Pitt had denied that war preparations were being made and on 25 May Talleyrand would obtain a declaration of England's neutrality. Nonetheless, George, wearing Henry VIII's armour, is prepared – this was the first print to hint at the possibility of war. Andromache was the wife of Hector and their parting before battle is a passage of great pathos in* The Iliad.

The GRAND REVIEW on SYDENHAM COMMON

*The Prince and his party were drove to the summit of a hill, where they made a stand for nearly an hour & a half, but where at length Obliged to retreat to the bottom setting fire to the furze & hedges the Smoke of which favoured their flight & left the several battalions masters of the field his Majesty followed the enemy on foot at the head of a troop of dragoons to the foot of the hill when he remounted & returned back to the Lines*

**The Grand Review on Sydenham Common**

28 June 1792

ISAAC CRUIKSHANK

On 23 June on Sydenham Common George reviewed the Coldstream and Grenadier Guards, which were under the command of his favourite son, the Duke of York. Here, supported by Pitt and Burke, he puts the revolutionary sympathizers – notably Fox and Sheridan, who is on the ground – to flight. The Prince of Wales is shown as their ally but this was unfair, since on 21 May he went to the House of Lords and spoke in support of a royal proclamation against seditious writings and meetings.

The King is depicted as the warrior leader of his country. In 1803, when invasion threatened, he attended an even larger rally in Hyde Park of 20,000 volunteers and was cheered by a crowd of over half a million.

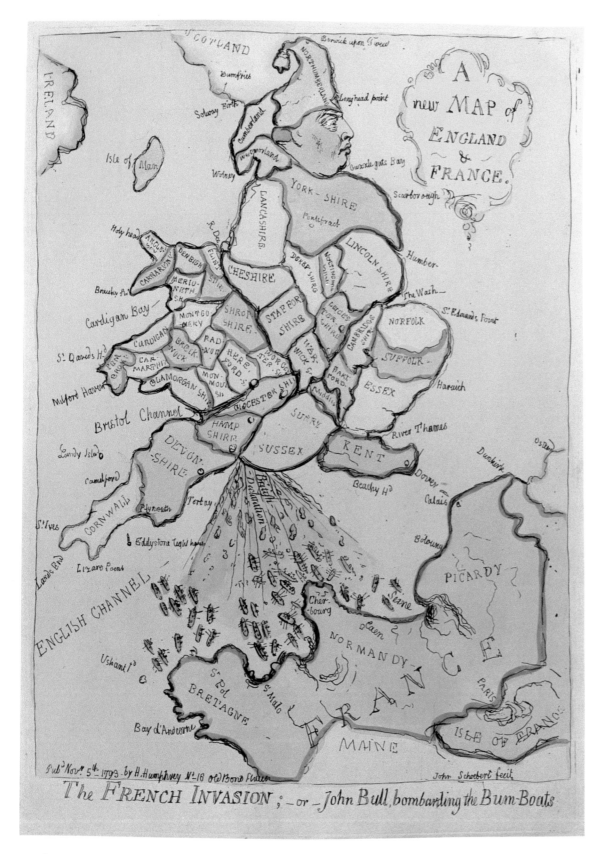

**The French Invasion; – or – John Bull bombarding the Bum-Boats**

5 November 1793

JAMES GILLRAY

*In the autumn of 1793 the French threw back the Austrians, Prussians, the English and the Spanish. Carrying the revolution to England was the declared policy of the republic, so George responds by directing a burst of shit to disperse the French invasion fleet. This is not a disrespectful print. George is now the very embodiment of England (and Wales, although not of Scotland), a bold determined figure protecting the country from the threat of invasion – just what his countrymen would expect and admire.*

*The transformation of George from a hesitant tyrant to a national emblem was now underway. He had been the subject of contempt or even hatred, but anger turned to gentle mockery, then gave way to respect and affection.*

## John Bull Humbugg'd alias Both Ear'd

12 May 1794

ISAAC CRUIKSHANK

The war against the French in Flanders is not going at all well and George does not know whom to believe. Pitt, armed with the ministerial paper, True Britton, like a newsboy blasts out the good news – 'Paris taken and more Cannon, Cartridge, Balls, Bombs & Assignats' – this referred to the Duke of York's defeat of French cavalry at Willems on 10 May. Fox, armed with the Whig paper, the Morning Chronicle, reports that 'the Combined Armies after a Severe Engagement were all Cut into Cabbage'. This news anticipated the defeat of the English and Austrian armies at the battle of Turcoing six days later.

'Both Ear'd' is a play on the word 'bothered', defined as 'being talked to at both ears by different persons at the same time, confounded, confused'. Bother also has the meaning of blarney or humbug. The news from Flanders was bad but pro-Pitt papers played that down.

His MAJESTY presenting an Elegant SWORD to ADMᴿ EARL HOWE.
As a token of Respect for the Services rendered his Country in the Glorious
Action with the French Fleet, on the 1ˢᵗ of June, 1794.
Published 25ᵗʰ Octᵇ 1794 by LAURIE & WHITTLE, Nᵒ 53 Fleet Street London.

## The Glorious First of June 1794

*The Terror was at its height in Paris; the French army was pushing
back the Austrians and the British (commanded by the Duke of York)
and was advancing towards Belgium; Pitt, fearful of radical uprisings,
suspended Habeas Corpus; and there were fears of invasion. Britain
needed some good news. That was provided by Admiral Earl Howe,
George's personal choice to command the Channel fleet. In searching
for a vital grain convoy coming from America to France, Howe learnt
that a French fleet had set sail from Brest in the middle of May to
meet it. On 28 May he came upon the French out in the Atlantic
and on 1 June in a battle off Ushant, Brittany, he inflicted a crushing
defeat on them. When Howe towed six captured ships into
Portsmouth there was national rejoicing – and the King, Queen and
Pitt joined in the celebrations: at last something to cheer about.
Nonetheless, the much-needed grain convoy arrived in France intact.*

Pub by W<sup>m</sup> Holland N 50 Oxford St Nov<sup>br</sup> 8<sup>th</sup> 1798

t shall disolve & like
of a Vision leave not
k behind

These Lands are mine
By Sycorax my mother

Paris

NCHANTED. ISLAND .

## Prospero on the Enchanted Island

8 November 1798

*Nelson's dispatches of his victory at the Battle of the Nile in August reached London on 2 October. It was called by Admiral Jervis 'the almost incredible and stupendous victory'. There was great national rejoicing and a spate of prints glorified Nelson. England is the enchanted isle of Albion where George tramples on the French flag; Caliban rages in Paris; and British ships tow the nine French vessels that were captured. Only two had escaped.*

## Bombardement des Trones de L'Europe

*c.* 1792

*The Spirit of the Revolution, standing on the bare bottoms of the National Assembly, administers a violent emetic to Louis XVI and directs the assembly's farts against the crowned heads of Europe, who cower while the Pope prays. The bare-breasted Catherine of Russia says she will kill all the assembly. George III is portrayed as half-blind and confused, begging Catherine to look after Hanover as he is 'deranged' and he hopes that war will be avoided by negotiation. This print asserts the confident commitment of the French to overthrow all monarchies.*

## The King of Brobdingnag and Gulliver

10 February 1804

JAMES GILLRAY

*Once again, Gillray turns to Swift, this time to belittle the French invasion threat. George and his family are watching a diminutive Napoleon sailing a boat, just as Gulliver's skills were laughed at by the King of Brobdingnag.*

Designed by an Amateur :— Etched by Jʳ. Gillray.

BDINGNAG and GULLIVER. (Plate 2ᵈ) Scene "Gulliver manœuvring with his little Boat in the Cistern, — Vide. Swifts Gulliver

version, as well as that of the Queen & her Ladies, who thought themselves well entertained with my skill & agility. Sometimes I would put up my Sail
rd & larboard; However, my attempts produced nothing else besides a loud laughter, which all the respect due to his Majesty from
n contain. This made me reflect, how vain an attempt it is for a man to endeavour to do himself honour among those, who are
or comparison with him ! ! ! See. Voyage to Brobdingnag

*s as tho a'd burst*
*ne of our Oxen tho.*

## The Emperor of the Gulls, in his Stolen Gear

28 May 1804

CHARLES WILLIAMS

*This is the first print to depict the swaggering Napoleon as emperor – a title bestowed on him by a subservient senate on 18 May. He was frequently called the Emperor of the Gauls but here 'of the Gulls' – those who had been duped by him. The Times called him 'an unprincipled and sanguinary usurper'. He had imitated 'by a splendid mockery, the long recognized, the consecrated and venerable institutions of the unpolluted honour of ancient states'. The daggers in the crown refer to the Duc d'Enghien, shot in March for plotting against Napoleon; and the dollars allude to France winning Spain as an ally. George dismisses the Emperor's pretensions: the French frog is no match for the British bull.*

## Pitt sur Georges observe l'Escadre Française

1805

*Between 1803 and 1805 there was a real threat of a French invasion. In July 1805, Napoleon had 90,000 men near Boulogne and 2,000 troop transport boats. This French print scoffs at the inadequate preparations of Pitt and the King. During the brief Peace of Amiens, 1802–3, Addington, who had taken over from Pitt in 1801, had cut the army and the navy, but war had resumed in May 1803 and on Pitt's return to office in April 1804 these cuts were reversed and 25,000 more militia were immediately recruited. The patriotic response was so great that there were not enough arms for all the volunteers. George took a keen personal interest in the military preparations, reviewing troops and giving his views on their deployment.*

Déposé à la B.ᵗ    *Pitt sur Georges observe l'Escadre Française.*    Chez Martinet.

*Folios of Caricatures lent out for the Evening*

*rofsly gulled twice or thrice over*
*entury, and under the same pretence of Refor...*

the navy increased in the same period from 16,000 to 140,000. In addition, from 1796 there were over 100,000 men in official militia units across the country and they served alongside private volunteer groups raised by the local gentry.

From 1798 to 1805 there were periodic threats of invasion from Napoleon, who made the French army the finest fighting machine in the world. There had been an attempted French landing in Ireland in 1796 and a French invasion force was sent to help the rebels in the Irish uprising of 1798. The fear of France entering Britain by the back door was one of the factors that led Pitt to pass the Act of Union between Britain and Ireland in 1800 – a union, alas, that was to cause two centuries of strife and bitterness.

Reading the novels of Jane Austen, suffused in rural tranquillity, it is easy to forget that in this period Britain was armed to the teeth in a life and death struggle with France. The greatest direct threat was posed in the years 1803–5 when Napoleon marshalled a large invasion force in northern France. In 1803, after war had started again following the brief Peace of Amiens, the government required local officials to interview every able-bodied male between the ages of seventeen and thirty-five to assess whether they could take up arms and defend their village or town. In southern England, the most vulnerable part of the country, at least half of those eligible were prepared to do that but further north enthusiasm waned: East Anglia was the most lukewarm. Nonetheless, 480,000 men pledged to fight if the country was attacked, supporting a militia that now numbered 176,000. Arthur Young asserted confidently in 1803, 'England can never be overrun….Her infantry is as numerous as her property is diffused.'

Britain's mobilization against the threat of invasion stimulated patriotic feelings and the caricatures reflect this: Britain is often depicted as a lion and France as a monkey. They proudly asserted that Britain stood alone defying a foreign tyrant. The King was not a distant figurehead: from 1803 every volunteer swore an oath of allegiance to him personally and the volunteers held parades to celebrate his birthday.

OUD'S_ over the Water to Charley_ a new Dramatic Peace now Rehearsing.

Pub.d April 5.t 1806

## Pacific Overtures – or – a Flight from St Cloud's over the Water to Charley – a new Dramatic Peace now Rehearsing

5 April 1806

JAMES GILLRAY

*Following the death of Pitt on 23 January, Fox became Foreign Secretary in Grenville's Ministry of All the Talents (depicted here as the 'broad bottom' orchestra in the foreground). He opened peace negotiations in March after the blows Napoleon had inflicted on the Third Coalition, particularly the brilliant victory at Austerlitz in December 1805. Gillray saw this as a Jacobin treachery. Napoleon's demands are outrageous: 'Dismantle your Fleet', 'Reduce your Army', 'Abandon Malta & Gibraltar'. George defiantly rejects them, 'We are not in the habits of giving up either Ships or Commerce or Colonies.'*

# 14 The Father Figure

GEORGE WAS OBSESSED with his position as the king. He fiercely protected the aura that surrounded his status and expected it to extend to his whole family. This meant that no man of the family should consider marrying a daughter from the English aristocracy – only foreign princesses carried the distinction he demanded. George's third brother, Henry, Duke of Cumberland (1745–90), was a rake who liked his mistresses to be lustful, his horses to be fast and his cards to be winners. He tutored the young Prince of Wales in the ways of the world. On 1 November 1771, while strolling with George in the woods around Richmond Lodge, Henry casually handed him a note informing him that he had married his mistress, the Hon. Anne Horton, a young widow who was the daughter of a Whig peer.

George, appalled at the news, banned his brother from court – which made Anne turn Cumberland House into a refuge for the Whigs where they could mock the piety of George and the greed of Charlotte. George wrote that a prince 'marrying a subject is looked upon as dishonourable.' Ominously he went on, 'I have children who must know what they have to expect if they should follow so infamous an example.'

Cumberland's marriage was the final impetus that led George to take active steps to prevent any of his children making an imprudent match. The Royal Marriages Act of 1772 made it illegal for members of the royal family under the age of twenty-five to marry without the consent of the sovereign. The die was cast. But the Bill had a rocky ride in the Commons: Edward Gibbon called it a 'most odious law' but observed, 'the King will be obeyed, and the Bill is universally considered to be his'. The Act would inflict misery and humiliation upon the

## The Humbug Wedding

1 August 1786

*RAMBLERS MAGAZINE*

*In December 1785, the Prince of Wales married in secret Maria Fitzherbert, a twice-widowed Roman Catholic. The marriage was eventually recognized by the Catholic Church but under English law it was invalid. By the Royal Marriages Act of 1772 children and descendants of the king had to obtain his consent to marry, up to the age of twenty-five, but, more importantly, the Act of Settlement of 1701 had debarred from the throne anyone who was a Catholic or who married a Catholic. News of the marriage leaked out into London society, but the Prince told his friends to deny it. As George and Maria were often together in public, the King and Queen must have learned about the marriage, although there is no official correspondence about its possibility. Here George and Charlotte surprise the couple in bed but George is carrying in his hand a copy of the Act of Settlement. This was yet another issue that drove the father and son apart.*

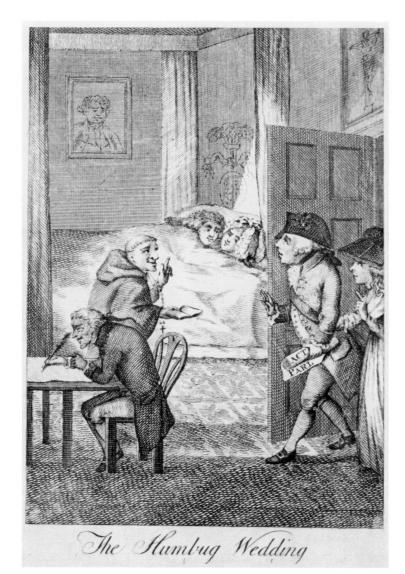

*The Humbug Wedding*

## A Milliner's Shop

24 May 1787

HENRY KINGSBURY

This charming scene of George and Charlotte visiting a milliner's shop in Windsor – which bears the royal warrant, 'Splitfarthing, Milliner to Her Majesty' – to buy hats, muffs and the fashionable extended petticoats for their daughters is accompanied by verses by Peter Pindar that poke fun at the parsimony of the royal couple. This outing for his daughters would have relieved the boredom of their Windsor life.

The modern Bard says Tom, sublimely sings
Of Virtuous, gracious, good, uxorious, Kings
Who love their Wives so constant from their Heart

Who down at Windsor daily go a shopping
Their heads so lovely into Houses popping,
And doing wonders in the hagling [sic] Art.

And why, in God's name, should not Queens & Kings
Purchase a Comb, or Corkscrew, Lace for Cloaks,
Edging for Caps, or Tape for Apron-Strings,

Or Pins, or Bobbin, cheap as other Folks.
Reader: to make thine Eyes with wonder Stare,
Farthings are not beneath the Royal Care!

lives of all George's daughters and draw resentment from his sons. It would also afflict royals of later generations.

Shortly after the Act was passed, George's second brother, William Henry, Duke of Gloucester (1743–1805), a weak wastrel, plucked up his courage to tell the King that he had secretly married his mistress, Maria, the humbly born Dowager Countess Waldegrave, in 1766 and that she was now pregnant. George banished him from court. So, at the age of thirty-four, George was estranged from his two surviving brothers, Prince Henry and Prince William. He now expected all his children, whom he loved when they were small, to be dutiful and bow to his will. He was a control freak and the control started at home.

A great deal is known about the daily habits of George and his family because Fanny Burney, the novelist, held the post of Second Keeper of the Robes to Charlotte. Beside her duties she kept a detailed record of court life, which was a rigid regime in which all knew their place and the exact time of each day when they had to perform their duties. There was no allowance for variation, and royal reproof was certain for anyone who failed to act exactly as he or she should. For the King's six daughters it was a daily struggle against boredom. Their letters reveal the dreary routine of walking with the King around Richmond, attending formal Drawing Rooms at St James's, endless evenings embroidering, drawing and playing cards – the dreary life of the underoccupied. When the King approached the door of one of his daughters' rooms he was preceded by a page who was not allowed to knock but had to make a little scratching noise. When the King appeared the princess had to stand up and speak only when her father spoke to her. Anyone in the royal presence had to withdraw by walking backwards.

### The Fair Quaker of Cheltenham

1788

*This is the only print that hints at a story in circulation for years, that in the 1750s, before he ascended the throne, George had an affair with a young Quaker called Hannah Lightfoot. Some accounts claim that he actually married her in 1759 and they had a son, and that she was later married off to a Mr Axford as a cover. Many historians have discounted the story but this print is interesting as it is evidence of the rumours about at the time. Some have even argued that George's guilt over this association was a contributory cause of his 'madness'. That is preposterous, but during his illness several of his ravings were about Quakers.*

Did you know the Lad that Courts you
He not long need sue in Vain.

Pub. Oct 2 1788 by S W

To CHELTENHAM SPA

Kingsbury

AIR QUAKER of CHELTENHAM.

Prince of Songs & Dance & Sports:
You Scarce will meet his like again. Midas

Nº3 Piccadily.

George and Charlotte had thirteen children who survived to adulthood and they are all listed in the List of Characters (pp. 216–18), but in this chapter I have focused only on some of the more interesting of their progeny.

### The Prince of Wales (1762–1830)

Hanoverian Princes of Wales had stormy relationships with their fathers. George III despaired at the profligate and licentious behaviour of his sons and in his eyes the worst was the Prince of Wales who ran up huge debts, had numerous affairs, gambled and drank to excess. George's rebukes were constantly ignored but in 1795 he insisted that the Prince should marry his cousin, Caroline of Brunswick. The Prince must get an heir, and upon his marriage Parliament would pay his debts; but it was a union made in hell. There were various attempts at reconciliation between father and son, and a meeting took place in 1804 but with little effect – the Prince was too much set in his ways, as was his father. The King made no attempt to introduce his son into the duties and responsibilities of kingship. The Prince was not shown any papers nor was his advice sought on any of the crises that afflicted his father.

### Augustus, Duke of Sussex (1773–1843)

Augustus, George and Charlotte's sixth son, was their only bookish child, and contemplated entering the Church. In southern Europe for his health, he fell in love with Lady Augusta Murray, the Earl of Dunmore's daughter, and married her secretly in Rome in 1793 without his father's permission. To

**The House of Hanover**

3 April 1788

*This rather charming print shows George in a favourable light as being disinterested in the Hastings diamond in the box marked 'B' for Benares and a bag of gold. (The trial of Warren Hastings had just opened.) The Queen on the other hand sings a ditty about the cash she loves; and the son and heir, the besotted Prince of Wales, revels in his secret slavery to the generously endowed Maria Fitzherbert.*

cement the union further, they went through another wedding ceremony at St George's Hanover Square on 5 December 1793, and on 13 January 1794 Augusta gave birth to a son whom they optimistically called Augustus. George III was told of his son's marriage by the Lord Chancellor on 24 January. He immediately insisted that the Chancellor, the Archbishop of Canterbury and the appropriate ministers should act to set the marriage aside – as the Prince was only twenty, it contravened the Royal Marriages Act. George also ordered that Lady Dunmore and her daughter should stay in England; Augustus had already returned abroad.

On 14 July the Arches Court of Canterbury declared the marriage null and void: Augustus was 'free from all bond of marriage with the said Right Honourable Lady Augusta Murray'. The child of the union, George III's first grandson, was thus made illegitimate. Augusta was given a pension by the King to live quietly at Teignmouth with her baby son. She briefly joined Augustus in Berlin in 1799 and they had a daughter, Augusta. He did then bend to his father's will and throw over Lady Augusta and by 1809 he had obtained control of his children, to whom he was an affectionate father.

This whole episode is another example of George III's stubbornness and his insistence that his will should always be obeyed. He could have given retrospective approval to this marriage even though it might have required some parliamentary adjustment to the Royal Marriages Act, but he was not even prepared to consider it. He wanted to ensure that as his son had married below his station, the offspring would never succeed to

*How pleasant is my dwelling place*

London Pub. by W. Holland. Oxford Street, May. 17.th 1792.

PSALM SINGING AT THE CHAPEL x x x x x

## Psalm Singing at the Chapel x x x x x [Royal]

17 May 1792

RICHARD NEWTON

*George owed his deep commitment to the Anglican Church to his mother, who urged him to be chaste, to honour marriage, and to involve his wife and children in the celebration of monarchy. At Windsor, there were daily prayers in St George's Chapel at 8 a.m., but it was so cold, to which George seemed impervious, that Charlotte and her daughters soon dropped out. However, on Sunday afternoons Charlotte read a sermon in English or German to her daughters. Here George and Charlotte, accompanied by their eldest daughter, the Princess Royal, and Princess Elizabeth, are singing with much gusto, 'How pleasant is my dwelling place.'*

the throne. There was no consideration of the feelings of either his son or his wife. George had to have his way.

### Elizabeth (1770–1840)

Princess Elizabeth was a victim of the torpor of the 'Nunnery', as the princesses sometimes called their home at Windsor. She was very stout and took a daily walk to try to reduce her weight. No suitable suitors were found and at the age of thirty-two she quoted an old ballad to her friend Lady Harcourt: 'Oh, how I long to be married, be married, before that my beauty decays.' Six years later the impoverished but handsome Louis Philippe, Duc d'Orléans, three years younger than Elizabeth, approached her. It was a move strongly supported by her brother the Prince of Wales, but Queen Charlotte dismissed the match: 'It can never be.' Poor, compliant Elizabeth accepted, saying, 'Without

## A Blow-up at Breakfast!

20 May 1792

RICHARD NEWTON

*On 9 May fear swept through the House of Commons when the lobby was filled with smoke and some thought it was a revolutionary conspiracy to blow up the House. The cause, however, was a pair of smouldering breeches that had been thrust into a closet. In rumour-rife London the blame was laid on radicals. Newton mocks that by suggesting the King's breeches were a target. The royal couple's simple breakfast of tea and muffins is disturbed.*

*A book published in 1821, after the King's death, recorded George's breakfast routine: 'When the King rises, which is generally half past seven o'clock, he proceeds immediately to the Queen's saloon, where His Majesty is met by one of the princesses.' Then George went to Divine Service for an hour, returning to the Queen's breakfasting room for a breakfast which lasted half an hour. 'The King and Queen sat at the head of the table and the Princesses according to seniority.' For his sixty-sixth birthday in 1804 the princesses gave him a silver-gilt egg-boiler complete with lamp and egg-timer.*

being a perfect good daughter, I never can make a good wife.' The family circle of George and Charlotte had managed to institutionalize unhappiness – the Queen's daughters were scared of her and her sons avoided her. In 1818, at the age of forty-seven, defying Charlotte's opposition, Elizabeth married Prince Frederick of Hesse-Homburg. Freed from the stifling atmosphere of Windsor and Kew they managed to have a happy life together.

### Sophia (1777–1848)

Sophia was the eleventh child of George and Charlotte. She was pretty but sickly and so short-sighted that her mother allowed her to wear unflattering spectacles. Unmarried, she gave birth to a boy, probably at Weymouth, on 5 August 1800 and he was baptized in the parish church there as Thomas Ward, a foundling.

He was later adopted by General Thomas Garth, a 56-year-old bachelor who was an equerry to George III. The general was short, his face disfigured with a dark red birthmark, and he was known for his old-fashioned manners and clothes – 'all powder and pigtails'. The story at court was that he had been the lover of the 22-year-old Princess. However, a rumour started to circulate that the real father of the child was her 29-year-old brother, Ernest, Duke of Cumberland (1771–1851). There was little firm proof but one of Sophia's other brothers, Edward, Duke of Kent (1767–1820), told Lord Glenbervie, a junior minister, that when Ernest had visited her, he 'took advantage of the family temperament in her…and got her with child'.

'Wicked Ernest' worked hard to secure his reputation. Scarred in the face as a soldier, he was remembered for his malicious wit, renowned for his extreme Protestantism and reviled for his racy and profligate life. Ten years after the event he twice told his aide-de-camp that he murdered his valet Sellis in 1810, and in 1830 he seduced Lady Graves, whose husband, a Lord of the Bedchamber, then cut his throat. To cap it all, there were rumours that Ernest was planning to have Princess Victoria, daughter of the Duke of Kent, done away with as she was the only person who stood between him and the throne.

### Amelia (1783–1810)

At the age of nineteen Princess Amelia fell in love with one of the King's equerries, General the Hon. Charles Fitzroy. At Weymouth they went riding together and she insisted upon playing cards at his table. This developed into a passionate and physical relationship – Amelia looked upon him as her husband – but it was concealed from the King. On reaching twenty-five, the age at which royal children no longer have to seek the statutory approval of the monarch to marry, she wanted to become his wife. In intimate letters she even expressed concern that her womb would not be strong enough to bear their children. But from 1808 Amelia's health declined due to tuberculosis. Two months before she died, she asked her doctor, the worldly Sir Henry Halford, to plead with her father for her marriage to Fitzroy, but he refused, saying it would endanger the King's health. On her deathbed, she said, 'Tell Charles I die blessing him.' Amelia was another victim of the narrow-minded selfish obstinacy of her parents.

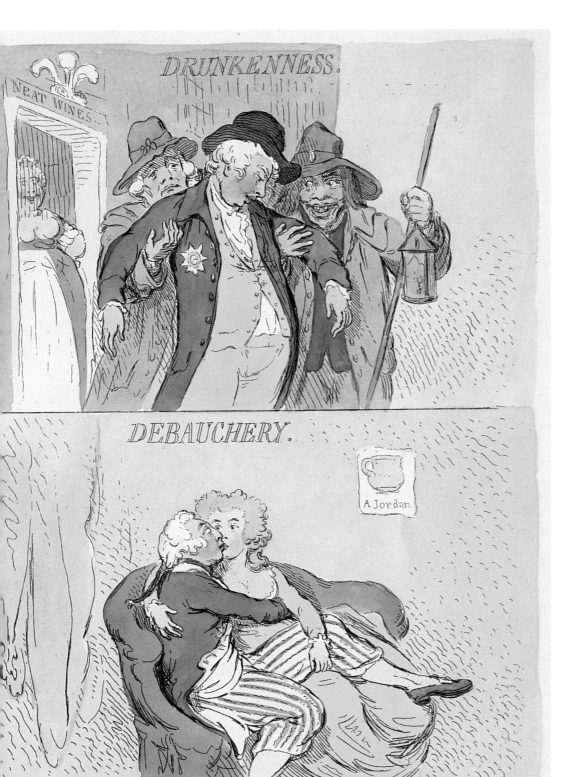

DRUNKENNESS.

NEAT WINES.

DEBAUCHERY.

A Jordan.

Pub.<sup>d</sup> May 24.<sup>th</sup> 1792. by H. Humphrey N.18. Old Bond Street

r PROCLAMATION.

...mation, is dedicated, as proper for imitation, and in place of the more dangerous Ones of Thinking.

## Vices overlook'd in the New Proclamation

24 May 1792

JAMES GILLRAY

*On 21 May a royal proclamation was issued for 'the preventing of tumultuous meetings and seditious writings' – its target being the revolutionary works of Tom Paine. Gillray points out that the vices of avarice, drunkenness, gambling and debauchery are still permitted and are practised by the royal family. The dangerous ones of thinking, speaking and writing are forbidden. He strikes again at the avarice of George and Charlotte, and as for their profligate sons: the Prince of Wales is helped home from a tavern by two watchmen; the Duke of York loses at the tables; and the Duke of Clarence fondles his mistress, the famous actress Dorothea Jordan. Gillray highlights the hypocrisy of the King's son, for the Prince of Wales, in his maiden speech in the House of Lords had actually supported the royal proclamation.*

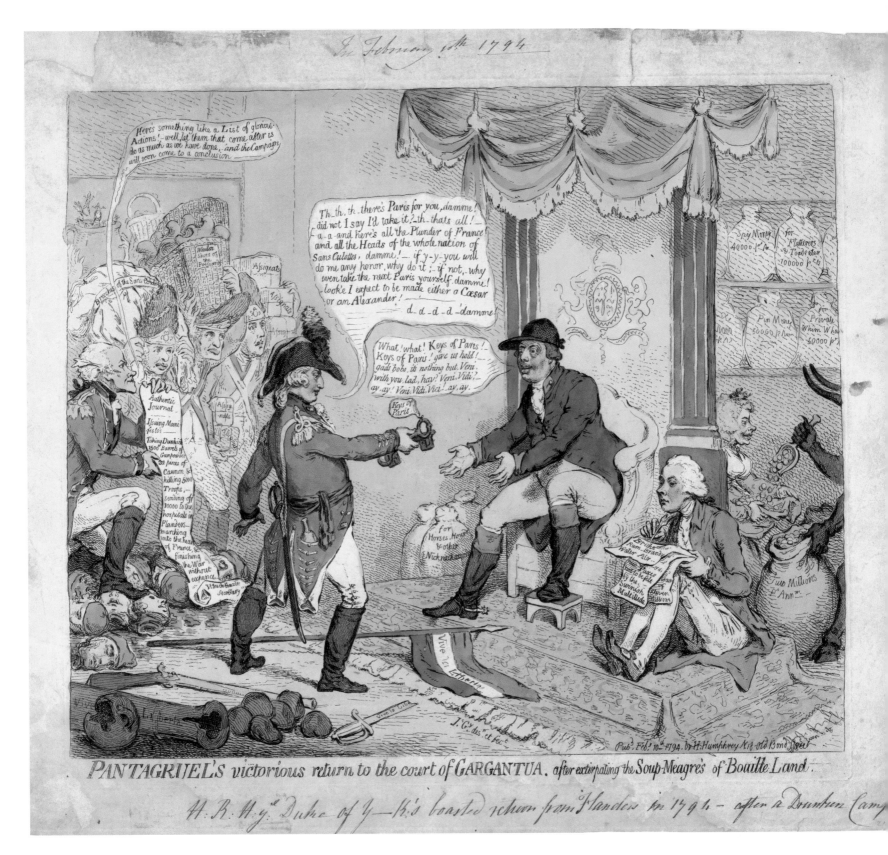

## Pantagruel's victorious return to the court of Gargantua

10 February 1794

JAMES GILLRAY

*George's second son, Frederick, Duke of York (1763–1827)
was commander-in-chief of the British army in Flanders
whose task was to resist the French invasion of Holland.
The campaign was disastrous. He failed to take Dunkirk
and had to retreat. The goggle-eyed King believes
anything his favourite son tells him – even that he had
captured Paris. The vain and bombastic York claims to
be Caesar or Alexander while poor Pitt bears a list of
taxes to pay for the campaign. On the Duke's return, Pitt
tried to have York sacked but his father wouldn't hear of
it and further reverses occurred for him in Flanders later
in 1794. Meanwhile, Charlotte rakes in the money from
the devil. In Rabelais's* Gargantua *Pantagruel is 'the all
thirsting one'. My copy of this print has written across
the bottom, in an 18th-century hand, 'H:R:H:y Duke of
Y—k's boasted return from Flanders in 1794 after a
Drunken Campaign'.*

## The Marriage of the Prince of Wales to the Princess of Brunswick

20 June 1795

*George III told his eldest son that he must marry, not
only to produce an heir but to provide an opportunity
for Parliament to pay off his debts. The King insisted
upon a German princess rather than a daughter of the
English nobility and chose his son's cousin, Caroline of
Brunswick. This engraving depicts the marriage in its
most favourable light and George III smiles benignly,
but he had made a disastrous choice. The Prince of
Wales was appalled at his first meeting with Caroline,
whom he found to be coarse, loud and rather smelly.
On the morning of his wedding on 8 April he told his
brother the Duke of Clarence, 'Tell Mrs Fitzherbert
she is the only woman I shall ever love.' As he walked
up the aisle he was quite drunk and had to be held up
by the Dukes of Bedford and Roxburgh. George
and Caroline probably slept together on only three
occasions but it was enough for a child to be conceived,
Princess Charlotte.*

THE MARRIAGE OF THE PRINCE OF WALES, TO THE PRINCESS OF BRUNSWICK,
*in the Chapel Royal at St. James's on Wednesday Evening 8th April 1795.*

Published 20th June 1795, by LAURIE & WHITTLE, 53, Fleet Street, London.

**John Bull ground down**

1 June 1795

JAMES GILLRAY

As part of the deal for marrying Caroline, commissioners were appointed to determine the total of the Prince of Wales's debts. It was over £630,000 (about £45 million in today's money), even though in 1787 and 1792 he had had debts paid off that totalled more than that. George III, depicted as a sun in the right corner, urges Pitt to go on grinding John Bull to pay off the debts as it is now 'for the good of your country? Hay? Hay?' The Prince fills his coronet with guineas showing them to his jockey Chifney (who had received a pension of £200 from him after he had been accused by Newmarket Stewards of pulling a race), a Jewish moneylender and Maria Fitzherbert. Edmund Burke, who had just received a royal pension, grovels with Henry Dundas for the guineas. George appears to condone the grinding down of the national interest to meet the profligacy of the Prince.

## Grandpappa in his Glory!!!

13 February 1796

*George always got on well with his daughter-in-law (and niece), Caroline of Brunswick. Four days after her marriage he was glad, in the absence of her disenchanted husband, to escort her as she walked on the terrace at Windsor. He was highly pleased when nine months later he received the news from his son of the birth of a daughter, who was christened Charlotte. George's daughter Elizabeth recorded, 'He talks of nothing but his granddaughter, drank her health at dinner and went into the Equerries' room and made them drink it in a bumper.' In this print George, with great affection, is feeding Charlotte, even though she is spitting most of it out. As she was second-in-line to the throne, George in 1806 assumed control over her education, removing her from her mother's house at Blackheath to Windsor. In 1810, when George succumbed to his final senility, Charlotte was still his only legitimate grandchild – though there were numerous illicit ones.*

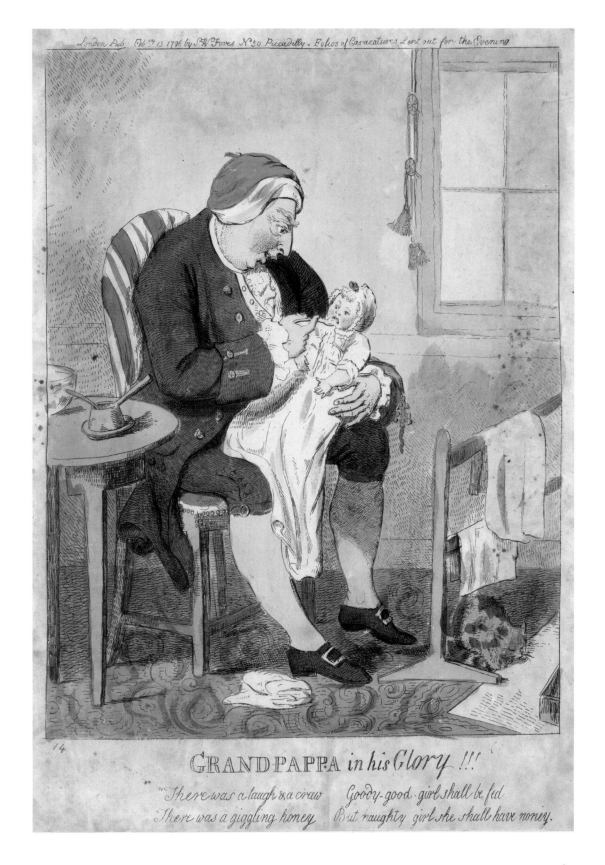

London Pub. Feb.ry 13 1796 by S.W. Fores N.o 50 Piccadilly. Folios of Caracatures Lent out for the Evening

GRANDPAPPA *in his* Glory *!!!*

"There was a laugh & a craw      Goody-good-girl shall be fed
There was a giggling honey      But naughty girl she shall have noney.

## La Promenade en Famille – a Sketch from Life

23 April 1797

JAMES GILLRAY

*George's third son, William, Duke of Clarence (1765–1837), was the oaf of the family. For twenty years, he had an affair with the popular actress and comedienne Dorothea Jordan, who bore him ten children – here three of them are being carted by their father to their home in Bushy Park. The fake coat of arms on the cart consists of a crown on top of a chamber pot, colloquially known as a 'jordan'. With the death of Charlotte, the Prince of Wales's only child, in 1817, there was pressure on George's other children to produce a legitimate heir and in 1818 William married a German princess. Dorothea died in poverty in France.*

J.ˢG.ʸ ad vivam fec.ʳ

*La Pro*

From Richmond
To BUSHY
Act III enter Little Pickle
de en Famille. — a Sketch from Life.
Pubd April 23d 1797. by H. Humphrey New Bond, & St James's Streets

## The Bridal Night

18 May 1797

JAMES GILLRAY

*George and the Queen, who is covered in jewelry, lead the bridal procession of their eldest daughter, Charlotte (1766–1828), demurely peeping from behind a fan. Her husband-to-be is Frederick, Duke of Württemberg, a widower with three children, who had a reputation for violence. He had abandoned his wife in Russia, where she had died, and initially George did not welcome him as a possible son-in-law. But Charlotte was prepared to have any suitable prince – Fanny Burney wrote that she wanted to escape from Windsor where she was 'in utter subjection for which she had neither the spirits nor the inclination'. Württemberg was so fat that Napoleon said of him, 'God put him on earth to see how tight you could stretch, without bursting.' The caricaturists dubbed him the great 'Bellygerent'. In this print Pitt carries a sack labelled £80,000, which was the bride's dowry and George insisted it be kept in England, claiming that was safer as there was a war on. In Germany Charlotte bore only a stillborn baby. A consolation was that in 1805 Napoleon made her husband King of Württemberg for switching to his side, so Charlotte became Queen – enraging her mother. Charlotte became just as fat as her husband and towards the end of her life had to be carried everywhere in a chair.*

Nibbling at a thin Slice of single Gloucester!!

## Nibbling at a thin Slice of single Gloucester!!

6 March 1798

*William Henry, Duke of Gloucester (1743–1805), George III's brother, evoked the King's anger through his secret marriage to Maria, Dowager Countess Waldegrave, which had taken place in 1766 but had to be revealed in 1772 when she became pregnant. Gloucester was a thin, timid, sickly, knock-kneed nonentity. By the 1780s he and Maria were leading separate lives and he took as his mistress a lady-in-waiting, Lady Almeria Carpenter, who was described as beautiful 'but to whom nature had been sparing of intellectual attractions'. She may well be the lady alluded to in this print.*

Marquis of Salisbury

LE TRIOMPHE DE L'AMOUR.

£80,000

Posset

*The* BRIDAL-NIGHT

Pub.ᵈ May 18ᵗʰ 1797. by H.Humphrey. 27 S.ᵗ James Street.

*London. Publish'd Nov.r 20.th 1804. by H Humphrey 27 St James's Str*

*Heaven — and before thee, and am no more worthy...*

*J. Gillray des & fec.*

The RECONCILIATION. — *And he arose and came to his Father, and his Father saw him, & had compassion, & ran, & fell on his Neck, & kissed him.* — Read the Parable Verse 16.th to 24.th

**The Reconciliation**

20 November 1804

JAMES GILLRAY

*The appalling relationship of the King and the Prince of Wales had been made public with the publication in 1803, at the insistence of the Prince, of their correspondence in which he begged for a military command, which the King firmly refused. The Prince also resented the regular and lengthy visits that his father paid to the Princess of Wales. They also disagreed about little Charlotte's education, which the King had taken in hand. Accordingly, the meeting had been postponed several times but was at last held on 12 November, when the Prince insisted upon the Queen and princesses being present. It was not an affectionate reconciliation. The stilted meeting began with the King saying, 'You have come, have you?' The verse at the bottom refers to the prodigal son.*

## The Prodigal Son

25 March 1809

ISAAC CRUIKSHANK

*In the past it had been the Prince of Wales, the reprobate, who was depicted as the Prodigal Son on the rare occasions when he was reconciled with his father, whereas Frederick, Duke of York was the King's favourite, whose military career he promoted. Now it is York, kneeling, stripped of all his military insignia, while the King says, 'Oh disgrace!! disgrace!!' York had to resign as commander-in-chief in March 1809 after a full Commons inquiry into allegations that he had profited from the sale of commissions and promotions by his former mistress, Mary Anne Clarke. He was actually acquitted of the charge but it was the sleaze scandal of the year – they were the victims of 121 prints, many of which depicted York as a dim-witted buffoon. George, once again let down by one of his sons, was appalled by both the alleged corruption and the public admission of York's adultery – he had had the added indignity of having his love letters read out in the Commons. Rumours spread that the Prince of Wales had encouraged the onslaught. Another brother, the Duke of Kent, had to go to the House of Lords to deny that he was involved. This incident produced a spate of attacks upon corruption in general. Nonetheless, York was reappointed commander-in-chief two years later in 1811.*

*The* PRODIGAL SON.

## Throwing the Stocking

April 1816

CHARLES WILLIAMS

*Princess Charlotte, newly married, waits in bed for the groom, Prince Leopold of Saxe-Coburg-Saalfeld, who is trying to get in through the door with her father, the Prince Regent. According to the old custom, the bride throws her stocking for luck to husbandless bridesmaids – here, four of George's daughters (watched by their décolleté witch-like mother) whose hopes of marriage have been dashed by their parents. Princess Augusta on the left says, 'We are all of the same flesh and blood, but stolen bread is always sweetest.' In 1812, at the age of forty-four, her wish to marry a royal aide-de-camp, General Sir Brent Spencer, had been rejected by her mother on the grounds of the King's madness: she may have married him secretly. The second sister is Princess Elizabeth who was courted at one point by Louis Philippe, Duc d'Orléans. Eventually, at the age of forty-seven she was to marry the gross, ugly and vulgar Prince Frederick of Hesse-Homburg. The stocking goes to the third sister, Princess Mary, who says, 'It's my turn next.' She was about to be married at the age of forty to her cousin, the insipid Prince William, Duke of Gloucester. The fourth is Princess Sophia who had given birth in 1800 to an illegitimate son, rumoured to have been fathered by her brother, 'Wicked Ernest', the Duke of Cumberland. Charlotte's marriage at last gave her aunts a chance of breaking free from their parentally imposed misery.*

Throwing the STOCKING.

## A couple of Humbugs

4 May 1818

*The buxom Princess Elizabeth, at the age of forty-seven, despite her mother's initial disapproval, was married at last on 8 April to the equally corpulent Prince Frederick of Hesse-Homburg. The press and the prints did not like him – he stank of tobacco from constantly smoking a meerschaum pipe and his face was covered with heavy whiskers and a moustache. Here a pipe is sticking out of his pocket. He was soon dubbed 'Humbug'. Napoleon's comment on this royal alliance was, 'The English royal family va incanagliarsi [lower themselves] with little petty princes, to whom I would not have given a brevet of sous lieutenant.'*

## The Hombourg Waltz, with Characteristic Sketches of Family Dancing!

4 May 1818

GEORGE CRUIKSHANK (KNAHSKIURC)

*This is a satire on the rush by several of the princes to find brides and beget legitimate heirs as a result of the death in 1817 of Princess Charlotte, the Prince of Wales's only child. Queen Charlotte is the shrouded figure on the right who watches a grossly fat Princess Elizabeth waltzing with her new husband, Prince Frederick of Hesse-Homburg. The Duke of Clarence on the left tells his brother the Prince Regent that he is having trouble finding a partner – but he had solved that by July when he married Princess Adelaide of Saxe-Meiningen. The Duke of York proudly struts past his diminutive wife who is finding solace in a pet dog. The Duke of Sussex in a tartan hat reflects on the fact that he had to abandon his wife, and his brother, the Duke of Kent, looks on contentedly as he is to be married on 29 May. The Duke of Cumberland, wearing a Hussar uniform, dances in another room as his mother refused to receive his wife at Court. A very happy family.*

**A Scene in the New Farce called the Rivals – or a Visit to the Heir Presumtive**

April 1819

CHARLES WILLIAMS

When Princess Charlotte died in childbirth in 1817 there was a rush to beget an heir as she was the only legitimate grandchild of George III. The Dukes of Clarence, Kent and Cambridge all married in 1818. On the left, the Duke and Duchess of Clarence look with envy on the Duke of Cambridge, whose wife had borne him a son, Prince George, on 26 March. The Clarences's daughter, also born in March, had survived only a few hours but he declares, 'I'll try again, & a boy too I'll warrant.' On the far right the Duchess of Cumberland tells her husband that they have but a small chance now. The winner, however, was a heavily pregnant Duchess of Kent, who on 24 May gave birth to Princess Victoria; she became Queen in 1837, due to her father's position in the line of succession. This is the first appearance in print of Victoria – albeit in embryo.

## A Voice from the Graves!!!

T. H. JONES

*Ernest, Duke of Cumberland (1771–1851) was the most vicious and vile of George III's sons. He became a soldier in Hanover and there he developed his life-long addiction to seducing whom he wished and bullying those he could. His valet, Joseph Sellis, was found murdered in 1810 in St James's Palace. Ernest later confessed to his aide-de-camp, under a strict oath of secrecy, that he killed him (a record of the confession is in the Royal Archives). Later Ernest caused the suicide – by razor – of the 2nd Lord Graves by seducing his wife. It is rumoured that he fathered the illegitimate son of his sister Princess Sophia. 'Wicked Ernest' came within a whisker of being the king of England: the only person who stood between him and the crown was little Princess Victoria. It was rumoured that he was plotting to push her aside or even to do away with her. How lucky we were!*

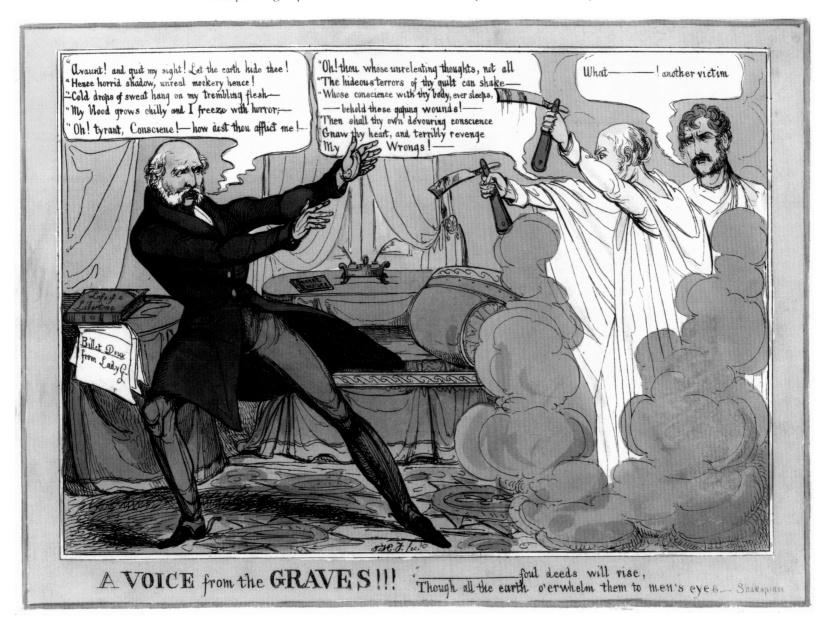

# 15 After Pitt

GEORGE III KNEW that he was on the throne because he was a Protestant and the grandson of a Protestant. The date of 1 August was celebrated as a public holiday as it was the anniversary of the accession of the first Hanoverian king, who succeeded in 1714 only because he was a Protestant. In a sermon preached before George I in 1715 a bishop declared: 'A Protestant country can never have stable times under a popish prince.' In 1715 and in 1745, Jacobites from Scotland had tried to overthrow the Protestant monarchy and restore the Catholic Stuarts. George was the head of the Church of England but the Protestant ascendancy was maintained throughout the country by squires and vicars, and George was determined not to let them down. His anti-Catholicism reflected the overwhelming view of his people.

Protestants believed that their freedoms had been won through their faith and that its continued observance protected them forever. It buttressed their pride and their confidence. Until the Catholic Relief Acts of 1778 and 1791, when a measure of reform was enacted, the long-standing Penal Laws meant that Catholics were excluded from the governance of the country: they were not allowed to vote or hold any civil office, nor sit in Parliament. They paid punitive taxes, could not possess weapons, and were barely allowed their freedom of worship. They were a persecuted minority.

### Integrity retiring from Office!

24 February 1801

JAMES GILLRAY

*Pitt's resignation on 3 February over Catholic emancipation had stung the country. Pitt, holding a document entitled* Justice of Emancipating Ye Catholicks, *leads out his ministers, who also carry various papers: Henry Dundas has* Advantages of the Union; *Grenville* Acquisitions from ye War: Malta, Cape of Good Hope, Dutch Islands [Ceylon]; *and Spencer Perceval holds* Enemies Ships Taken & Destroyed. *It was an impressive record of a successful government that was not acknowledged by the bigotry of the King. The usual rabble of Whigs cry out for office but they too were to be disappointed.*

INTEGRITY retiring from Off

TREASURY.

*"Men, in conscious Virtue bold,"*    *"Nor heed the Mob's tumultuous cries,*
*"Who dare their Honest purpose hold.*    *"And the vile rage of Jacobins — despise.*

THE HONORS of the SITTING!! a Cabinet Picture.

## The Honors of the Sitting!! A Cabinet Picture

30 January 1805

CHARLES WILLIAMS

*Addington had resigned as First Lord of the Treasury nine months before this dinner took place. It was a great honour, since the only other Prime Minister to dine tête-à-tête with the King had been Lord Bute. When Addington left office the King wished to make him an earl, which he declined, but he did accept the offer to continue to live at White Lodge in Richmond Park. In 1805, when this print was published, he joined Pitt's ministry as Viscount Sidmouth and Lord President of the Council. The delicacies on the cake stand are in the shape of crowns and coronets. Pitt looks through the window incredulously rather than jealously, since he had no interest in acquiring a title for himself; he preferred to give titles to people whose support he could then rely upon.*

## Mort de Pitt, 1806

*The news of Napoleon's devastating destruction of the Russian and Austrian armies at Austerlitz on 2 December 1805 reached London on 1 January 1806. This was the final blow to Pitt whose health was already breaking down – weak, emaciated and racked by stomach ulcers from his lifetime addiction to port wine, his frame simply could not take any more. He died at his house on Putney Heath on 1 January 1806. In this French print, the devil claims him and George III, virtually blind and no longer supported by Pitt's leading reins, is about to stumble over a sack of his government's crimes into the abyss. In French eyes, it was Pitt who was leader of the coalitions against them; George was simply a figurehead, uttering as he falls, 'Goddam je suis f…'*

### The Honey Moon

February 1806

CHARLES WILLIAMS (?)

*Following Pitt's death George had to appoint a Whig government and that meant Fox returning to office as Foreign Secretary. Princess Augusta wrote that the King 'showed considerable uneasiness of mind', but with no other option, he graciously greeted his erstwhile foe: 'Mr Fox, I little thought you and I should ever meet again in this place. But I have no desire to look back upon old grievances, and you may rest assured I shall never remind you of them.' Sheridan plays the fiddle; Lord Derby a pipe and tabor; and Fox dances with Britannia. The honeymoon was short – by September Fox was dead, and seven months after that George dismissed his Ministry of All the Talents.*

Following the Irish rebellion of 1798, which had brought fears that France would use Ireland as a launch pad for an invasion, Pitt decided that the Irish problem could be resolved by abolishing the Irish Parliament; establishing a legislative union by a United Kingdom of Great Britain and Ireland; and granting Catholic emancipation to win over the Catholic majority in Ireland. Removing the restrictions would mean that Irish Catholic MPs could sit in the House of Commons.

Pitt believed the nation's security required the whole Irish population to be bound into the new United Kingdom – the Act of Union was passed in 1800 and took effect on 1 January 1801. He moved quite cautiously, however, in proposing that Catholics be allowed to hold public office by the repeal of the Test Act. He knew it would be difficult to obtain the King's agreement. George held that his coronation oath was inviolable. He had sworn to maintain the rights and privileges of the Anglican Church and to exclude Roman Catholics from any position of authority under the Crown. He told his family that if he ever abandoned the oath 'I am no longer legal Sovereign of this country'. There was no power on earth that would absolve him from 'the due observance of every sentence' of the oath. He said he had discussed the matter with lawyers, religious scholars and bishops, and it was a matter 'beyond the decision of any Cabinet of Ministers'.

Pitt might have persuaded the King, although unlikely, if he had had a united Cabinet. Unfortunately for him, the ministers were divided and in particular the Lord Chancellor, Loughborough, a Portland Whig who had ratted upon one party, was preparing to rat again. Pitt had still not made the King fully aware of his intentions about relieving the Catholic disabilities when Loughborough is said to have alerted George to what was afoot.

At the levee on 28 January 1801 George exploded over the issue of Catholic emancipation; he told Dundas: 'I shall reckon any man my personal enemy who proposes any such measure.' This was similar to the form of words he had used to bring down the Fox–North coalition in 1783. On 31 January Pitt wrote at length to the King setting out the case for Catholic emancipation and making it clear that if the King did not agree he would resign. He added a gentle rebuke about the use of 'Your Majesty's name to influence the opinion of any individual'. George replied that his 'sense of religion, as well as political duty' prevented him from 'discussing any proposition tending to destroy this groundwork of our happy constitution'. This flat rejection was unacceptable to Pitt. His pride was hurt,

*Why, these Hungry Rats thought to have had some fine pickings, I warrant, but egad they'll be woundedly mistaken, tho' they seem to want it nationly; but that dam'd Scotchman carried off a rare lot of it & as to poor Billy the Butler why he was so fond of a drop of black strap, that when he and his friends, got at it, d'ye see, the rest of the Servants did as they pleased, poor Rogues I'se afraid they'll undermine the Barn they're so main Hungry.*

RATS in an Empty Barn.

Folios of Caricatures lent out for the Evening

## Hungry Rats in an Empty Barn

March 1806

CHARLES WILLIAMS

*When the Ministry of All the Talents, or broad-bottomed government, took office in February 1806 the Whigs had not been in power for nearly thirty years and all their factions expected positions. There were the Grenville family, radicals such as Sir Francis Burdett, and the followers of Fox. Grenville is sniffing at an upturned Treasury tub; Grey scampers towards a lantern; the red-nosed Sheridan races towards a candle and Fox nibbles at a pile of sacks. Here they are fruitlessly searching the country's food store, which George tells them is empty – stripped clean during the years under Pitt.*

### An Ever-Green!!!

3 April 1806

JOHN CAWSE

*The title of this elongated, spare figure of Pitt, which appeared some two months after his death, echoes the belief of Pittites that his memory and influence would live on. But the print reflects two points of view: note the guillotine and gallows.*

### L'Ambition le domine

November 1806

TOUZEL

*In 1805, Pitt fashioned the Third Coalition against France, and Prussia joined the alliance the following year. This French print reflects Napoleon's accusation that Britain was 'buying Prussian blood'. Ambition, as a naked woman, lashes the tiger, George III, promising him that 'This is just an account'. The Prussian king has a bloody nose – Napoleon had just crushed his army at Jena – and a swift-footed Mercury offers more gold to the hesitant Tsar Alexander. The jibe was unfair as the broad-bottomed ministry was averse to foreign subsidies.*

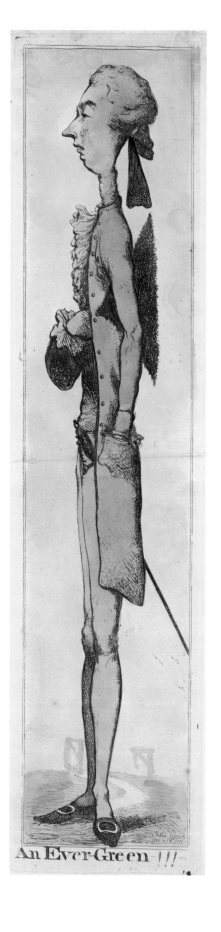

## The Pigs Possessed: – or – The Broad bottom'd Litter running headlong into ye Sea of Perdition

18 April 1807

JAMES GILLRAY

*For a variety of reasons Grenville's government wished to make a limited concession towards the Catholics. In early March, it moved a Bill to open all ranks in the army and navy to Catholics. When first mooted, the idea was to bring England into line with Ireland, where an Act of 1793 had opened up the military to the rank of colonel (army) or captain (navy), and the King had reluctantly agreed to that. When it was apparent that the proposal meant Catholics could become generals, the King made it clear he could not accept the measure. This and some unrest in the government's own ranks, which the Tories cleverly exploited, led the government to withdraw the Bill. George demanded a pledge from his ministers that they would never raise the Catholic issue again: a quite improper and unconstitutional demand. The government rejected it and the King dismissed them, which led to a surge of popularity for him. Here Farmer George drives the 'broad bottom'd' pigs out of office, declaring that he did not want them if 'the Pope has got possession of you all': Grenville hits the waves first; Charles Grey, the Foreign Secretary, floats on his back. The last one to leap is Sheridan, who was reluctant to surrender his seals of office as Treasurer of the Navy.*

his authority diminished and his position undermined. Accordingly, he resigned on 3 February but remained in office to deliver the budget. In March, the Speaker of the House (and son of one of George III's doctors), Henry Addington, took over as First Lord of the Treasury.

Pitt had underestimated the King's reaction; he did not handle the dissidents in his Cabinet well; and he probably believed that on this issue, as with all the others in the previous seventeen years where George's views collided with his own, his will would prevail. Moreover, he did not want to let down his closest political allies – Cornwallis, who as viceroy had handled the union with Ireland, Castlereagh, Canning, Dundas and Grenville – who were all committed to Catholic emancipation.

The main fault, however, was not Pitt's. The legal advice to George was that Catholic emancipation would not undermine or devalue his coronation oath – but George simply ignored it. All George's stubbornness and lack of imagination, which had led to the loss of the American colonies, came into play again. It is barely comprehensible that he could so quickly and so lightly dispose of a great Prime Minister who had served him so well; who was facing a major crisis in the continental war as Britain was isolated, standing alone against France; who was having at the same time to cope with a crippling shortage of food throughout the country; and who was also recovering from a breakdown in his own health in the previous autumn. For Pitt it was not only a matter of Catholic emancipation. He was not prepared to allow the King to interfere in a policy that was crucial to his government: he could no longer tolerate George's incessant interference in all matters of state. George found a crutch to lean on in Addington, 'My dear Addington, you have saved your country', but the wit's verdict was:

> Pitt is to Addington
> As London is to Paddington

Pitt returned to office in 1804 to deal with the renewed threat from Napoleon, but in January 1806 his fondness for port finally killed him. He was followed by a Whig government – the Ministry of All the Talents under Lord Grenville – but when in 1807 they in turn moved to grant greater freedom to Catholics, George sacked them. He declared: 'I can give up my crown, and retire from power. I can quit my palace and live in a cottage. I can lay my head on a block and lose my life, but I cannot break my coronation oath.'

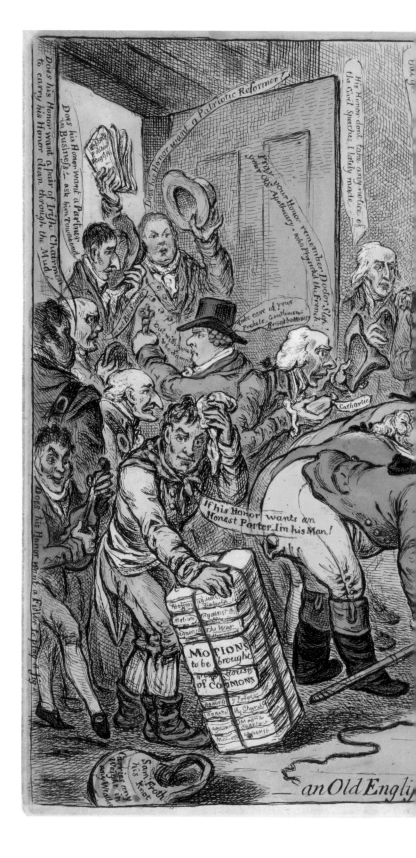

ntleman pester'd by Servants wanting Places.

Pub.ᵈ May 16.ᵗ 1809 – by H. Humphrey 27 S.ᵗ James's Street –

*After the fall of the Ministry of All the Talents in 1807, the Duke of Portland once again took office as First Lord of the Treasury (he had briefly held the post in 1783), but it was a weak administration and by the time this print was published rumours were circulating of a possible new administration. All the excluded gather to press their case: on the left is Grenville's Broad Bottom'd faction; on the right are George Tierney, the Duke of Bedford, Sheridan and Grey (the greyhound); and at the back are the radicals William Cobbett and John Horne Tooke. Just to the right of the King stands Portland, supported at the elbow by Spencer Perceval and they both ignore Grey. Perceval became Prime Minister when Portland resigned that autumn. George, peering through his eyeglass, rejects all their pleadings. This is the last caricature that Gillray did of George. The King was an old man, virtually blind: he did not even notice when his pen had run out of ink, and his writing, once small and neat, had become large and straggly.*

# 16 The Final Years, 1811–1820

IN THE AUTUMN OF 1810 news of Princess Amelia's declining health (she died on 2 November) finally turned George's muddled mind. Princess Elizabeth wrote that 'his excess of feeling has been too much to bear'. At the end of October Lord Wellesley, the Foreign Secretary, waiting to see the King, heard him sobbing: 'a sort of wailing, most horrible and heartrending to hear.' Robert Willis was summoned with his straitjacket and the King had to be placed under restraint. In October and November it became clear that he could no longer conduct government business and on 20 December Spencer Perceval, the Prime Minister, introduced a Regency Bill. The Prince of Wales was sworn in as Regent on 6 February 1811.

George's sanity vacillated for a few months – sometimes he was able to ride out at Windsor and the princesses visited him. Each day a report on his condition was sent to Charlotte and each week he was seen by a small committee of councillors to determine his condition. They came to the conclusion that he could never resume his royal functions. He lived in the northern apartments at Windsor, separate from his wife and daughters, and after June 1812 Charlotte never bothered to visit him again. The pattern of the earlier relapses returned – talking incessantly, imagining strange happenings, believing George I was still alive, and arranging marriages, such as the Princess of Wales to the Duke of Clarence, who were then to go to Botany

**George the – IIIrd – aged – 72– 1810**

25 October 1810

ROBERT DIGHTON

*This print by Dighton, a fan of the royal family, celebrates George's golden jubilee as monarch. The date was celebrated in over six hundred places in England, in Scotland and Wales, and in the far-flung outposts of the British Empire. In the City of London, the Lord Mayor organized fireworks and celebrations in the streets, and the pillars at the front of the Mansion House were decorated with a huge crown. It was the first time that a royal event of this kind had ever happened. The nation rejoiced and gave thanks for the survival of their king: he had overcome a grave illness; had become the emblem of unbeatable Britain' when threatened with invasion; had not succumbed to lust or lavish living; and had re-established the reputation of the monarchy. It was a personal triumph – he was loved, respected and revered. But it was at the close of the jubilee year that George succumbed to his last long illness.*

Pub.ᵈ Octᵣ 25ᵗʰ 1810.

George the-IIIʳᵈ-aged-72-1810.
REIGN'D-50-Years. A ROYAL JUBILEE.
Taken at Windsor    by R Dighton, Spring Gardens

Stop, Stop Stop Brother Jonathan, or I shall fall with the loss of blood— I thought to have been too heavy for you— But I must acknowledge your superior skill — Two blows to my one!— And so well directed too! Mercy mercy on me, how does this happen!!!

Ha—ah Johnny! you thought yourself a *Boxer* did you!— I'll let you know we are an *Enterprizeing* Nation, and ready to meet you with equal force any day.

W. Charles del et Sculp

A BOXING MATCH, or Another Bloody Nose for JOHN BULL.

## A Boxing Match, or Another Bloody Nose for John Bull

1812

WILLIAM CHARLES

*British children have no knowledge of the War of 1812 between America and Britain, for it was a sideshow to the conflict with Napoleon. American children, on the other hand, know a great deal: a British army burnt the White House in Washington; an American army successfully defended Baltimore, an event which gave birth to the Star-Spangled Banner; and Andrew Jackson took a step towards the presidency by successfully defending New Orleans.*

*America declared war on 18 June 1812 to secure, in the words of former President Jefferson, 'the final expulsion of England from the American continent'. This meant Canada,*

*but in a series of battles and skirmishes little was won and for a time Detroit was lost to the British. The 1814 peace treaty restored all captured land to both sides, so nothing was gained.*

*I believe that this is the first time this print and the one on p. 212 have been published in England. They are by William Charles (1776–1820), who was born in Edinburgh but worked in New York and Philadelphia. He was America's first great satirist and famous for his images of this war. Although George was no longer the effective king, it was still his image rather than that of John Bull which represented Britain. He was not forgiven for the American revolutionary wars.*

**John Bull making a new Batch of Ships to send to the Lakes**

1814

WILLIAM CHARLES

*In 1812, the tiny American navy did well, but in 1813 the British fleet asserted its supremacy at sea. The battles on the lakes inland were different. In 1813, the British were defeated on Lake Erie, which allowed the Americans to drive them out of Detroit. On 11 September 1814, the fleet accompanying a large British army advancing into New York from Canada was defeated at Plattsburgh on Lake Champlain by Captain Macdonough – referred to in this print – and the British had to retreat. George III is still represented as the villain of the piece.*

Bay in Australia. He also believed that his son Octavius, who had died in childhood, was alive but all his other sons were dead. The King refused to be shaved and henceforth grew a long straggling beard. He walked around his rooms in a purple flannel dressing-gown and an ermine nightcap, spending hours tying and untying his handkerchiefs, buttoning and unbuttoning his waistcoat. Every afternoon he changed for dinner, wearing his Orders right up to the day he died.

After the Queen's death in 1818 the Duke of York took over responsibility for the care of his father (granted £10,000 a year to do so). In about September 1819 he found him 'playing on the harpsichord and singing with as strong and firm a voice as ever I heard'. But by the end of the year the King was so emaciated and weak that York did not expect him to live much longer. By that time George was deaf as well as blind. On one occasion he talked for fifty-eight hours with barely a break; he could not sleep and was physically exhausted. In January 1820, his fourth son, Edward, Duke of Kent, died suddenly at Sidmouth but George was incapable of understanding this. On the 29th of that month his own long painful journey came to an end.

From the onset of the King's last illness in 1811 until his death, Charlotte and her family had to bear the cost of his medical care. The Queen's secretary protested that physicians would charge up to 30 guineas for a visit. During the earlier bouts of illness Willis had received £1,000 a year for twenty years. By 1820, the total spent on the King for medical reasons since 1812 was £271,691. 18s. (£19 million). This significantly reduced the amount of money that George and Charlotte left to their children.

George II's funeral had been virtually ignored but when George III died, although he had not appeared in public for ten years, 30,000 people travelled to Windsor to what was supposed to be a private family funeral. The nation had come to realize that during his reign the Crown had drawn closer to the people – *The Times* editorial on the day of his funeral declared: 'It is an important truth that most of the qualities which George III possessed…were imitable and attainable by all classes of mankind.' A new type of monarchy had been created.

**George the Third, 1820**

*This is the only print of George III enduring his last long period of insanity. It was a melancholy and lonely end.*

## Funeral Procession of George III

1820

*The funeral took place on the evening of Ash Wednesday, 16 February 1820. Throughout the day at Windsor guns were fired at five-minute intervals and the mourning bells tolled. The coffin was brought into St George's Chapel at 9 p.m. to the strains of Handel's* Dead March; *six dukes, led by Wellington, were the pallbearers; and ten marquises carried the canopy. The chief mourner, on the right, was the Duke of York; George IV was dangerously ill with pleurisy. The Garter King of Arms, Sir Isaac Heard, who had been one of the heralds who proclaimed George king in 1760, and who was now nearly ninety, read out his titles for the last time.*

Cruikshanks del.

FUNERAL P

# List of Characters

**Addington, Henry, first Viscount Sidmouth** (1757–1844) A great survivor. Speaker of the House of Commons (1789–1801), Prime Minister (1801–4), then Home Secretary (1812–21). He was created Viscount Sidmouth in 1805 when he briefly joined Pitt's last ministry. A reactionary Protestant whose anti-libertarian Acts derived from his network of spies. His father, Anthony Addington, was a doctor who attended Lord Chatham and George III; thus in the prints Addington frequently carries a clyster pipe used for administering enemas.

**Amelia, Princess** (1783–1810) The youngest daughter of George III. From the age of fifteen she was her father's favourite. At nineteen she fell in love with one of the King's equerries, General the Hon. Charles Fitzroy, and considered herself his wife. She never asked for her parents' approval, knowing it would not be forthcoming, and sadly succumbed to tuberculosis.

**Augusta, Princess of Wales** (1719–72) Daughter of Frederick II, Duke of Saxe-Gotha-Altenburg. Married in 1736 to George II's son, Frederick, Prince of Wales (1707–51), and gave birth to the future George III in 1738. After her husband's death she appointed Bute to be George's tutor – a disastrous choice that led to rumours of his being her lover. As a result she became a figure of derision, attacked as power-hungry and sinister. These criticisms were undeserved.

**Augusta, Princess** (1768–1840) Second daughter of George III. The most extrovert of the brood, she fell for an aide-de-camp, General Sir Brent Spencer, and they may have been secretly married. She nursed her mother in her final illness.

**Burgoyne, General John** (1723–92) 'Gentleman Johnny.' His attitude to the war in America was 'gung-ho'. In 1777, he led a British army down from Canada into New York State. He took possession of Fort Ticonderoga, but three months later, outnumbered by the Americans, he surrendered at Saratoga. He returned home in disgrace, joined the Opposition, but from 1783 dropped out of politics and turned his talent to writing plays, including *The Heiress*, which was translated into several foreign editions.

**Burney, Fanny** (1752–1840) Novelist, playwright, diarist and voluminous letter-writer. Daughter of the musical historian Charles Burney. From 1786 to 1791 she was Second Keeper of the Queen's Robes but maintained her friendship with the royal family thereafter. Her diaries reveal the boring, tedious and dull nature of the regime that Charlotte and George inflicted upon their daughters. In 1793, she married a French émigré soldier and became known as Madame d'Arblay.

**Burke, Edmund** (1729–97) Anglo-Irish politician, orator and philosopher. A Whig close to Fox and Sheridan, he drafted the Government's India Bill in 1783 and urged the impeachment of Warren Hastings. He was an early critic of the French Revolution and quarrelled with Fox and the Whigs after his great work, *Reflections on the French Revolution*, was published in November 1790; it became one of the philosophical texts of Toryism.

**Cambridge, Prince Adolphus, Duke of** (1774–1850) Seventh son of George III. A soldier in the Hanoverian and British armies, he was made a field marshal in 1813. In 1818, he married Princess Augusta of Hesse-Cassel. His granddaughter, Mary of Teck, married King George V.

**Canning, George** (1770–1827) Brought up in Whig circles, he was converted to Toryism by William Pitt at the time of the French Revolution and became the poet and wit behind the fortnightly Tory magazine, the *Anti-Jacobin*. He bribed Gillray to be kinder to his close friend Pitt, but was always suspected of being too liberal not least because of his dedication to the cause of Catholic emancipation. He held junior posts in Pitt's administrations and refused office under Addington and Lord Grenville. He was Foreign Secretary 1807–9 and 1822–27 and briefly Prime Minister in 1827. He died in office.

**Charlotte, Princess Royal, Queen of Württemberg** (1766–1828) Fourth child and eldest daughter of George III. Her father rejected several potential husbands and reluctantly agreed in 1797 to her marrying the immensely fat Duke of Württemberg. She lived mainly in Germany and in 1805 became Queen of Württemberg when Napoleon made her husband King for switching sides. She became fatter than her husband and by the age of sixty she had to be carried in a chair.

**Charlotte, Queen** (1744–1818) Princess of Mecklenburg-Strelitz, she married George III at seventeen in 1761 and bore him fifteen children (of which thirteen survived to adulthood). A plain, dull and dutiful wife who had a penchant for jewelry and snuff.

**Clarence, Prince William, Duke of,** later **William IV** (1765–1837) George III's third son who joined the navy as a midshipman at the age of thirteen and served in the West Indies. He was always distant from George. For twenty years he had a relationship with the famous actress Dorothea Jordan, who bore him ten children. Following Princess Charlotte's death there was pressure to produce a legitimate heir to the throne and in 1818 William married the austere but home-loving Princess Adelaide of Saxe-Meiningen, but their two baby girls died in infancy. He succeeded his brother George IV in 1830 and was known as the Sailor King.

**Clarke, Mary Anne** (1776–1852) In 1803, she became the mistress of Frederick, Duke of York. He was commander-in-chief and in 1809 she was accused of selling commissions and he of colluding. The money served as revenue for the financially embarrassed Duke and his expensive mistress.

**Cornwallis, Charles, first Marquis Cornwallis** (1738–1805) He was a successful general in the American Revolutionary Wars but was trapped at Yorktown in 1781 by a Franco-American force and had to surrender. That was the end for Britain. He went on to serve as governor-general of India and then viceroy and commander-in-chief in Ireland, where he suppressed the rebellion in 1798 and helped to carry the Act of Union in 1800. He resigned in 1801 over the King's refusal to grant Catholic emancipation. He died in India shortly after arriving for a second term as governor-general.

**Cumberland, Prince Ernest, Duke of** (1771–1851) Fifth son of George III. Known as 'Wicked Ernest' – the prints convey the popular conviction that he had murdered his valet and fathered a child by his sister Princess Sophia. He had military training in Hanover and served under his elder brother the Duke of York in Flanders in 1793–5 during the war against the French. He became a field marshal in 1813 and two years later married Frederica, daughter of the Grand Duke of Mecklenburg-Strelitz. His mother opposed the match, even though the bride was her niece. He became King of Hanover in 1837 as under Salic Law, which prevailed there, Victoria could not succeed to the throne.

**Dundas, Henry, first Viscount Melville** (1742–1811) Scottish lawyer and politician who was Pitt's drinking companion and closest friend. In Pitt's ministries he was Home Secretary (1791–94), Secretary of War (1794–1801) and First Lord of the Admiralty (1804–5). He became Viscount Melville in 1802. In 1806, he was impeached by the Commons, but not by the Lords, for misappropriating naval funds. He was acquitted but it finished him and he never held office again.

**Elizabeth, Princess, Landgravine of Hesse-Homburg** (1770–1840) Third daughter of George III. Physical and sensual, as well as large, she yearned to get married but her mother refused a series of suitors, including Louis Philippe, the future King of France. She eventually escaped the 'Nunnery' in 1818, at the age of forty-seven, by marrying the equally stout Prince Frederick of Hesse-Homburg – their remaining life together was happy.

**Fox, Charles James** (1749–1806) Charismatic leader of the Whigs and the first Leader of the Opposition. He rose to fame by criticizing North's conduct of the American war but formed a coalition with him in 1782–83. Loathed by George III, he became the Prince of Wales's closest political friend. His support of the French Revolution helped to keep the Whigs out of office. For a few months he was Foreign Secretary in Lord Grenville's Ministry of All the Talents and moved the abolition of the slave trade a few days before his death.

**Francis, Sir Philip** (1740–1818) He is thought to be the author of the vitriolic Junius letters, published in 1769–72, which poured scorn on Grafton and North. In 1774, he arrived in India as one of the councillors of the governor-general, but he soon clashed with Warren Hastings and was later injured in a duel with him. Upon his return to England in 1781 he entered Parliament, became a strong Foxite and was one of the prime instigators of the impeachment of Warren Hastings.

**George, Prince of Wales,** later **George IV** (1762–1830) Eldest son of George III. His profligate and licentious behaviour outraged his father. In 1762, he married his cousin Princess Caroline of Brunswick, but it was a disaster. Although nearly made Regent in 1788–89, he did not assume this role until 1811 and ruled for the rest of George III's reign.

**Grafton, Duke of** (1735–1811) A follower of Chatham, he was First Lord of the Treasury 1766–70. He liked fast horses and fast women but lacked charm. His period of office was troubled by the problem of John Wilkes. Rightly the main victim of Junius's letters.

**Grenville, George** (1712–70) Prime Minister 1763–65. He fatally insisted on Parliament's right to tax the American colonies and introduced the infamous Stamp Act in 1765 – taxation without representation. It was also during his ministry that the House of Commons voted to expel John Wilkes. Grenville's verbosity and desire to have his way in patronage matters irritated George, who dismissed him.

**Grenville, Lord** (1759–1834) Son of George Grenville and cousin of William Pitt the Younger. He was Home Secretary (1789–91) and Foreign Secretary (1791–1801) under Pitt and as Prime Minister led the Ministry of All the Talents (1806–7).

**Kent, Prince Edward, Duke of** (1767–1820) George III's fourth son. Lived largely abroad, often to avoid creditors. In 1818 he cast aside his mistress of more than fifteen years, married a German princess and fathered the future Queen Victoria. He died when she was just eight months old, six days before his father.

**Mary, Princess** (1776–1857) Possibly the most attractive of all the royal daughters, she was able to escape from the 'Nunnery' only by marrying her cousin, William, Duke of Gloucester (1776–1834), in 1816 at the age of forty. Gloucester was described by a contemporary as 'a good man, but amazingly stupid, tiresome and foolish'. He was preoccupied with his status, resenting the fact that he was not allowed the title His Royal Highness. However, on his marriage he not only got that title but was also made a field marshal. Of all George's children, Mary lived the longest. There are photographs of her in the 1850s with her niece Queen Victoria, who came to look upon her 'as a sort of grandmother'.

**Montagu, John, fourth Earl of Sandwich** (1718–92) A gambler, rake and member of the Hell-Fire Club of distinguished, debauched grandees. He was dubbed 'Jemmy Twitcher', after a character in Gay's *Beggar's Opera*, for ditching his old friend John Wilkes in 1763. First Lord of the Admiralty in the years 1771–82, he bears much of the blame for Britain's naval failure in the American War of Independence. He gave his name to the English language for inventing a snack to be served at the gaming tables.

**Murray, William, first Earl of Mansfield** (1705–93) Lord Chief Justice from 1756 to 1788, he was the most famous judge of the 18th century. An avowed enemy of John Wilkes. His judgment in the Somersett Case in 1772 ended slavery in England: 'The black must be discharged.' Macaulay termed him 'the father of modern Toryism'.

**North, Frederick, Lord** (1732–92) MP for Banbury at 22, junior Lord of the Treasury at 27, Chancellor of the Exchequer at 35, a post he retained for 13 years, combining it with that of Prime Minister from 1770 to 1782. Held responsible for precipitating the Boston Tea Party in 1773, which ultimately led to the loss of the American colonies. Neither he nor the King can be absolved for that humiliating loss. He could not survive the defeat at Yorktown in 1781. He destroyed his reputation by entering into a brief coalition with Fox, his great parliamentary accuser, in 1783. Affable, plump and at home in the Commons, he was no war leader. Horace Walpole said of him: 'Though his country was ruined under his administration, he preserved his good humour.' Often referred to as Boreas, Greek god of the North wind, in the caricatures.

**Norton, Sir Fletcher** (1716–89) Attorney General 1763–5 and Speaker of the House of Commons 1770–80, but without any of a Speaker's qualities for he was provocative, unmannerly, short-tempered and choleric. A supporter of North and a persecutor of Wilkes, he switched to Fox. He was known to the caricaturists and pamphleteers as 'Sir Bullface Doublefee', a reference to his greed and to his appearance.

**Perceval, Spencer** (1762–1812) A protégé of Pitt. Attorney General under Addington and Pitt, Chancellor of the Exchequer under Portland and Prime Minister 1809–12. Supported Wellington in the prosecution of the Peninsular War. Known as 'Little P' – he was castigated as 'a little man with a little mind' – and for being the only Prime Minister to be assassinated – shot by a madman in the lobby of the House of Commons.

**Pindar, Peter** (1738–1819) The pseudonym (after the Greek poet) of John Wolcot, a Devon doctor and clergyman. He came to London in 1781 and made a living from satirical verses, his most popular target being George III. His *Ode upon Ode* of 1787 enjoyed an enormous vogue. As the King became more popular Pindar targeted Pitt, but it was never the same and by 1805 his witty edge had disappeared.

**Pitt, William, the Elder, first Earl of Chatham** (1708–78) An outstanding orator and one of the great Prime Ministers of the 18th century. Established British control over India, Canada and many West Indian islands. A great promoter of British commerce – beloved by the City; mistrusted by George III; suffered from depression bordering on madness.

**Pitt, William, the Younger** (1759–1806) The second son of Lord Chatham. Became Prime Minister in 1783 at the age of twenty-four and held office through a time of much difficulty and peril. He resigned in 1801 when George III refused to consider Catholic emancipation following the Act of Union with Ireland. Recalled in 1804, he died in office in 1806.

**Portland, Duke of** (1738–1809) Prime Minister of the notorious Fox–North coalition for nine months in 1783. A leading Whig, he joined Pitt in 1794 and was Home Secretary until 1801. Although deaf, gouty and infirm he was recalled as Prime Minister from 1807 to 1809 but it was a weak ministry. Prints depict him as grey as Portland stone.

**Pratt, Sir Charles, first Earl Camden** (1714–94) Appointed Attorney General in 1757, Chief Justice of the Court of Common Pleas in 1761 and Lord Chancellor in 1766 (to 1770), he was a key figure in the Chatham faction. Famous for his 1763 judgment in the case of John Wilkes that general warrants were illegal. He opposed the British policy in America.

**Rockingham, second Marquis of** (1730–82) Prime Minister 1765–66 and from March 1782 until his death in July. In 1766, he repealed the Stamp Act but was dismissed when George wanted Pitt the Elder to come back. He had little political experience and needlessly alienated the King. In opposition he supported proposals to grant independence to the American colonies. He was Edmund Burke's patron, helping him to a seat in Parliament.

**Shelburne, second Earl of** (1737–1805) Prime Minister for a few months in 1782–83 but he resigned when the Commons rejected his peace terms ending the American war. Too arrogant to consider himself a member of a party, he was distrusted as an intriguer, gaining the nickname 'Malagrida' (a Portuguese Jesuit who had been convicted of heresy). Caricatured in prints as swarthy, sly and devious.

**Sheridan, Richard Brinsley** (1751–1816) Playwright, wit and politician. His renowned eloquence was used to damn Warren Hastings and to promote the Whigs. Fox's greatest friend and confidant of the Prince of Wales. Treasurer of the Navy in the Grenville's Ministry of All the Talents. He was manager of the Drury Lane Theatre when James Hadfield tried to assassinate George III there in 1800. Always depicted in prints with a large, mottled nose.

**Sophia, Princess** (1777–1848) Fifth daughter of George III. Unmarried, but in 1800 she had an illegitimate son. General Thomas Garth, a 56-year-old equerry to George III, was said to be the father, although there were rumours that her brother Ernest, Duke of Cumberland had fathered the child.

**Stuart, John, third Earl of Bute** (1713–92) George's tutor and closest friend as Prince of Wales. Influential on George's interests as a patron of the arts and sciences. Once king, George insisted Bute join the Cabinet and he become First Lord of the Treasury in 1762. It was tragic for both of them – George was seen as a puppet and Bute was satirized as the lover of the King's mother. He did not like the job – he was a born courtier, not a politician – and after a year he scuttled out of office. From 1766 he was excluded from the King's circle.

**Sussex, Prince Augustus, Duke of** (1773–1843) Sixth son of George III. The only one of the children to have an academic interest. Sent to study abroad, he fell in love with Lady Augusta Murray and married her without his father's consent. Although they had two children, George III insisted on having the marriage declared null and void, making his grandchildren illegitimate.

**Thurlow, Lord** (1731–1806) Attorney General 1771–8 and Lord Chancellor 1778–83 and 1783–92. Instrumental in bringing down the Fox–North coalition in 1783, he came to believe he was irreplaceable. He intrigued with the Prince of Wales against Pitt, who sacked him in 1792, threatening to resign if the King did not support the decision.

**Townshend, Charles** (1725–67) Capable minister and good orator. As Chancellor of the Exchequer in 1767 he introduced the so-called Townshend Acts which imposed import duties on certain items in America – and alienated the colonists. Townshend died suddenly shortly after introducing the measures.

**Wilkes, John** (1725–97) A rake on the make who became a folk hero. Founded the *North Briton* in 1762; his attack on the King in No. 45 in 1763 led to his arrest on a charge of libel. Years of government persecution followed and the denial of his election as MP in 1768. 'Wilkes and Liberty!' was the public cry but he ended up as Lord Mayor of London in 1774 and an MP from 1774 to 1790 – a respected figure of the Establishment.

**York, Prince Frederick, Duke of** (1763–1827) Second son of George III. He married his cousin, Princess Frederica of Prussia in 1791 but they soon amicably separated. Commanded the British troops in the disastrous Flanders campaign of 1793–94. Commander-in-chief 1798–1809. Resigned because he was accused of colluding with his mistress in the traffic of military promotions. Reinstated 1811. An inveterate gambler – he was usually in debt. The closest of the family to George, he took over his care in 1818 when the Queen died.

# Chronology

1738 *4 June*. Birth of Prince George William Frederick, future George III

1751 *March*. Upon the death of his father, Frederick, Prince of Wales, George becomes Prince of Wales

1760 *25 October*. Death of George II and accession of George III

1761 *8 September*. Marries Charlotte of Mecklenburg-Strelitz
*22 September*. Crowned in Westminster Abbey

1762 *May*. Earl of Bute appointed First Lord of the Treasury
*12 August*. Birth of George, Prince of Wales (later George IV)

1763 *February*. Peace of Paris ends Seven Years War
*April*. George Grenville succeeds Bute as First Lord of the Treasury
*23 April*. Wilkes publishes No. 45 of the *North Briton*
Birth of Prince Frederick (later Duke of York)

1765 Stamp Act passed
Grenville replaced by Marquis of Rockingham as First Lord of the Treasury
Birth of Prince William (later Duke of Clarence and William IV)

1766 Rockingham sacked and Duke of Grafton appointed First Lord of the Treasury
Birth of Charlotte, Princess Royal (later Queen of Württemberg)

1767 Townshend's import duties in America
Birth of Prince Edward (later Duke of Kent)

1768 Wilkes stands for election
George helps to found the Royal Academy of Arts
Birth of Princess Augusta

1770 *January*. Grafton resigns. Lord North appointed First Lord of the Treasury
*March*. British troops kill 5 in Boston
Birth of Princess Elizabeth (later Landgravine of Hesse-Homburg)

1771 Birth of Prince Ernest (later Duke of Cumberland)

1772 *February*. Death of George III's mother, Augusta, Princess Dowager of Wales
Royal Marriages Act

1773 *16 December*. Boston Tea Party
Birth of Prince Augustus (later Duke of Sussex)

1774 Birth of Prince Adolphus (later Duke of Cambridge)

1775 *19 April*. The first skirmishes of the American War of Independence at Lexington and Concord

1776 *4 July*. American Declaration of Independence
Birth of Princess Mary (later Duchess of Gloucester)

1777 *17 October*. Burgoyne surrenders at Saratoga
Birth of Princess Sophia

1777 Catholic Relief Act

1779 Birth of Prince Octavius (died 1783)

1780 Gordon Riots
Birth of Prince Alfred (died 1782)

1781 *19 October*. Cornwallis surrenders at Yorktown

1782 *March*. Marquis of Rockingham succeeds North as First Lord of the Treasury
*July*. Rockingham dies and is replaced by the Earl of Shelburne

1783 *April*. Fox–North coalition takes office led by the Duke of Portland
*September*. Treaty of Versailles recognizes American independence
*December*. India Bill founders and George III dismisses coalition
Pitt the Younger appointed First Lord of the Treasury
Birth of Princess Amelia

1788 Impeachment of Warren Hastings
George's first serious attack of 'madness'

1789 *February*. George recovers and the Regency Bill is withdrawn
*14 July*. Storming of the Bastille in Paris

1790 *November*. Publication of Burke's *Reflections on the Revolution in France*

1792 *21 May*. Royal proclamation against seditious meetings and writings

1793 *21 January*. execution of Louis XVI
*1 February*. France declares war on Britain

1794 Whigs under Portland defect to Pitt

1795 *8 April*. Prince of Wales marries Princess Caroline of Brunswick
*October*. King's coach attacked
Gagging Acts passed

1796 Birth of Princess Charlotte, daughter of the Prince of Wales

1798 Rebellion and French landing in Ireland

1801 *1 January*. Union of Great Britain and Ireland as the United Kingdom
George's second attack of 'madness'
*February*. Pitt resigns over Catholic emancipation. Henry Addington appointed First Lord of the Treasury

1802 Treaty of Amiens with France

1803 Renewal of hostilities between Britain and France. Threat of invasion

1804 George's third attack of 'madness'
Pitt returns as First Lord of the Treasury

1805 *21 October*. Battle of Trafalgar

1806 *23 January*. Death of Pitt
George appoints the Ministry of All the Talents under Lord Grenville
*13 September*. Death of Charles James Fox

1807 Grenville's ministry falls over Catholic emancipation. Portland appointed First Lord of the Treasury

1809 Spencer Perceval appointed First Lord of the Treasury

1810 *25 October*. King's golden jubilee
*November*. Princess Amelia dies. Onset of King's final illness

1811 *6 February*. Prince of Wales sworn in as Regent

1815 *18 June*. Battle of Waterloo

1817 *November*. Death of Princess Charlotte

1818 *November*. Death of Queen Charlotte

1819 *24 May*. Birth of Princess Victoria of Kent (later Queen Victoria)

1820 *29 January*. Death of George III at Windsor
*16 February*. Funeral and interment at St George's Chapel, Windsor

# Further Reading

Ayling, Stanley, *George the Third*, London, 1972

—, *Fox, The Life of Charles James Fox*, London, 1991

Black, Jeremy, *George III, America's Last King*, New Haven and London, 2006

Brooke, John, *King George III*, London, 1972

Cannon, John, (ed.), *The Letters of Junius*, Oxford, 1978

Carretta, Vincent, *George III and the Satirists from Hogarth to Byron*, Athens, Georgia and London, 1990

Cash, Arthur H., *John Wilkes: The Scandalous Father of Civil Liberty*, New Haven and London, 2006

Clarke, John, *The Life and Times of George III*, London, 1972

Colley, Linda, *Britons, Forging the Nation 1707–1837*, New Haven and London, 1992

Ditchfield, G. M., *George III, An Essay in Monarchy*, Basingstoke, 2002

Foreman, Amanda, *Georgiana, Duchess of Devonshire*, London, 1999

Fortescue, Sir John (ed.), *Correspondence of King George the Third from 1760 to December 1783*, London, 1927–28 (6 vols)

Fraser, Flora, *Princesses: The Six Daughters of George III*, London, 2004

Hague, William, *William Pitt the Younger*, London, 2004

Hibbert, Christopher, *George III, A Personal History*, London, 1998

Hobhouse, Christopher, *Fox*, London, 1934

*The Letters of Horace Walpole*, London, 1840

Marsden, Jonathan (ed.), *The Wisdom of George III*, London, 2005

Mitchell, Leslie, *The Whig World: 1760–1837*, London, 2005

Pares, Richard, *King George III and the Politicians*, Oxford, 1970 (first published 1953)

Plumb, J. H., *England in the Eighteenth Century*, Harmondsworth, 1968 (first published 1950)

—, *The First Four Georges*, London, 1956

—, *Men and Places*, London, 1963

—, *Royal Heritage: The Story of Britain's Royal Builders and Collectors*, London, 1977

Roberts, Jane (ed.), *George III & Queen Charlotte: Patronage, Collecting and Court Taste*, London, 2004

Thomas, Peter D. G., *George III, King and Politicians, 1760–70*, Manchester, 2002

Tillyard, Stella, *A Royal Affair*, London, 2006

Wardroper, John, *Wicked Ernest*, London, 2002

—, *Kings, Lords and Wicked Libellers: Satire and Protest, 1760–1837*, London, 1973

Weintraub, Stanley, *Iron Tears: America's Battle for Freedom, 1775–1783*, London, 2005

Wilson, Ben, *The Laughter of Triumph: William Hone and the Fight for the Free Press*, London, 2005

Wright, Christopher, *George III*, London, 2005

# Picture Credits

# Index